THE GURU GUIDE™ TO TIME MANAGEMENT:

Advice from the World's Top Experts

JOSEPH H. BOYETT, PH.D.
JIMMIE T. BOYETT

Authors of the *Guru Guide* Series

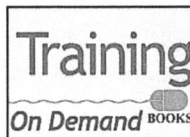

Training
On Demand BOOKS

CONTENTS

INTRODUCTION

One day a young man went to his boss to ask for a day off. His boss' reply expresses what many of us feel about not having enough time. Sometimes it seems like we don't have enough time to take even one day off.

EMPLOYEE: I would like to take the day off tomorrow if I could. I've got some personal things I need to get done. Is it okay?

BOSS: "So you want a day off. Let's take a look at what you are asking for. There are 365 days per year available for work. There are 52 weeks per year in which you already have 2 days off per week, leaving 261 days available for work. Since you spend 16 hours each day away from work, you have used up 170 days, leaving only 91 days available. You spend 30 minutes each day on coffee break which counts for 23 days each year, leaving only 68 days available. With a 1 hour lunch each day, you used up another 46 days, leaving only 22 days available for work. You normally spend 2 days per year on sick leave. This leaves you only 20 days per year available for work. We are off 5 holidays per year, so your available working time is down to 15 days. We generously give 14 vacation days per year which leaves only 1 day available for work and I'll be darned if you are going to take that day off!" (*http://www.ahajokes.com/off05.html*)

It is a funny story, but all too true. There never seems to be enough time to get everything done.

One of the reasons you have chosen to read this book is probably that you feel something is just not right in your personal and/or work life. Maybe you feel rushed most of the time. Maybe you are constantly under stress. You work hard, but still you can't seem to get things done on time. Many things that are important to you are not done at all or aren't done as well as you would like. Maybe you have a bad case of what Connie Merritt, author of *Too Busy for Your Own* Good, calls "Busyness."

DO YOU HAVE A BUSYNESS PROBLEM

Connie Merritt says "busyness" is the "soft addiction" today. Being busy can give you a psychic and physical boost, at least for a time, a high not unlike the high a drug addict feels. However, like the drug addict, the busyness high passes and then you must feed it with even more busyness. She offers a "busyness" quiz in her book that you might want to take if you get a chance. You can find in on pages 6-8 of her book.

Here are some of the things Merritt includes in her quiz. Merritt says you may have a "busyness" problem if you:

- Are working hard, but don't seem to ever get caught up with work;
- Skip meals or eat on the run;
- Miss family events because of work;
- Are always multitasking;
- Feel out of control;
- Often lose or misplace important items and documents;
- Are frequently grumpy and short tempered;
- Have difficulty sleeping;
- Take telephone calls from work at all hours;

- Skip or forget appointments; or

- Constantly tell people how overworked you are.

(Merritt 2009, pp. 6-8)

Richard Luecke, author of *Time Management*, says you may have a bad case of the Merritt's busyness, or at least a problem with managing your time if:

- You are impatient for the elevator door to close;

- You are obsessed with recalibrating your watch;

- You eat lunch at your desk and often resort to carry-outs for dinner; or

- When responding to a personal or family crisis, find yourself thinking, "This is really going to wreak havoc with my schedule."

(Luecke 2005, p. xvii)

Steve Prentice, author of *Cool Time*, adds that you may be too busy if:

- You line your office wall with sticky note reminders of things you have to do;

- You can't leave the office without carrying a stack of work home with you;

- You have the urge to work weekends, even when no one is forcing you to do so;

- You constantly feel burned out, angry, worried, and often can't sleep.

(Prentice 2005, pp. 10-11)

4....Joseph H. Boyett & Jimmie T. Boyett

Rita Emmett, author of *Manage Your Time to Reduce Your Stress*, says you may be suffering from busyness if:

- You think you have to be available 24/7;

- Your job requires you to travel a lot more than you want;

- You are working longer hours and carrying more responsibility than you think is good for you

(Emmett 2009, pp. 34-35)

How did you do? Did any of Merritt, Luecke and Prentice and Emmett's busyness indicators apply to you? Are you too busy? Are you even in the danger zone of busying yourself to distraction? You CAN do something about it.

You want to be happier, less stressed and more in control of your life. You are not alone. Unfortunately, most of us feel that way at one time or another. We feel that we are suffering from a "lack of time," a "time famine." We need help in managing our time.

A lot of time management help is available. There is no shortage of advice on the topic of time management. If you go to Amazon.com and search for books on the topic, you will get a list of over 100,000. If you search Google for websites dealing with time management, you will get more than 1.5 million hits. There is not a lack of advice. In some ways, there is too much advice. Wouldn't it be nice if you could find a good summary of the best time management advice available? Suppose you could read one book that would compare and contrast the best advice from the world's greatest time management experts. Well, you've found that book. *The Guru Guide to Time Management* provides a clear, concise and informative introduction to the wisdom of the world's top time management advisors.

Obviously, we cannot cover every "expert's" advice on time management in this book. What we can do and will do is summarize what we consider the best tips, tools, and techniques for time management available today from the world's top time management experts— our gurus. Some of these tools, tips and techniques may not apply to you or work for you, but we are convinced that many will. Here is the best advice from the most well known experts today on how to improve your life and work performance by doing a better job of managing your time.

OUR GURUS

In selecting our gurus, we began by consulting with our friends and associates, asking them whose advice about time management they had found most helpful. We searched the mainstream press and online social media to find out what journal articles, books and blogs on time management people were reading and talking about. We asked who the popular media—TV, radio, business periodicals and blogs—were citing on time management issues. Who was widely recognized as THE authority on time management? Who was gaining recognition? Who were the pundits quoting? Whose ideas were being discussed?

We narrowed down our list to the following 25 gurus whom we think offer some great time management ideas. They are:

- Dave Allen, author of Getting Things Done

- Samantha Ettus, author of The Expert's Guide to Doing Things Faster
- Rita Emmett, author of Manage Your Time to Reduce Your Stress
- Tom Fabrizio and Don Tapping, authors of 5S for the Office
- Sandra Felton and Marsha Sims, author of Organizing Your Day
- B. Eugene Griessman, author of Time Tactics of Very Successful People
- Patricia Haddock, author of The Time Management Workshop
- Edward M. Hallowell, author of Crazy Busy
- John Hoover, author of Best Practices, Time Management
- Regina Leeds, author of One Year to an Organized Work Life
- Richard Luecke, author of Time Management
- Alec Mackenzie and Pat Nickerson, authors of The Time Trap
- Connie Merritt, author of Too Busy for Your Own Good
- Julie Morgenstern, author of Time Management from the Inside Out and Making Work Work
- Steve Prentice, author of Cool Time
- Roberta Roesch, author of Time Management for Busy People
- Lee Silber, author of Time Management for the Creative Person

- Elaine St. James, author of Simplify Your Work Life

- Brian Tracy, author of Time Power and Eat That Frog

- Michelle Tullier, author of The Complete Idiot's Guide to Overcoming Procrastination

- Donald E. Wetmore, author of The Productivity Handbook

- Jan Yager, author of Creative Time Management for the New Millennium

We hope you will find the time to read the books and articles on time management written by our gurus. They have much, much more to offer you than the ideas we are able to cover in this book.

ORGANIZATION OF THIS BOOK

We have designed this book to be your reference manual for managing your time. It is organized around key time management issues our gurus agree are important. We cover each issue in a separate chapter and present the best thinking of our panel of time management gurus about that issue. We show you where our gurus agree and disagree. When our gurus offer different approaches, we illustrate and explain the differences.

The Guru Guide to Time Management consists of this introduction and six chapters:

Chapter One: Time Management Basics: In this chapter, you will learn some truths about time management and barriers that our gurus say most people face in getting control of their time. Finally, we will introduce you to four steps that our gurus say you need to follow to get control of your life and better manage your time.

Chapter Two: Set Your Personal Goals and Priorities. Our gurus teach us that time management isn't about GETTING MORE THINGS DONE. It is about GETTING MORE OF THE IMPORTANT THINGS DONE. Therefore, step one in learning to manage your time involves deciding what is important TO YOU. What do YOU want to accomplish with your life? We'll provide some exercises in this chapter our gurus offer to help you start sorting out what really matters TO YOU.

Chapter Three: Identify Your Time Wasters. Time Wasters are those things, habits and people who are getting in the way of you achieving your goals. In this step, you will learn how to keep and analyze a guru-approved time log in order to identify your biggest time wasters, including things such as: interruptions; having to attend meaningless meetings; poor management of phone calls, email or internet usage; procrastination, and so on.

Chapter Four: Deploy Time Management Tools and Techniques. In this step, we cover eight proven time management tools and techniques that our gurus say you can deploy to begin eliminating your most troublesome time wasters that you identified in Chapter 3.

Chapter Five: Get and Stay Organized. One of the biggest time wasters for most people is lack of organization. In this chapter, we will show you how to employ a five-step process to bring order into your life that our gurus say really works.

Chapter Six: Sustain. We offer some final thoughts on perhaps the most important piece of time management advice our gurus have to offer.

YOU JUST MIGHT LEARN A LOT

One final note before we begin. One of our gurus, Brian Tracy says this about why you should read his book *Time Power*:

"If you were to read this book on time management and incorporate the very best ideas contained here into your ways of living and working, you could double your productivity, performance and output"

(Tracy Time Power 2007, p. 82)

If Tracy is right, think about the kind of increase in productivity, performance and output you could obtain by reading and adopting the best ideas of not just one time management guru but of the 25 covered in this *Guru Guide to Time Management*.

10....Joseph H. Boyett & Jimmie T. Boyett

CHAPTER ONE:
SOME TRUTHS ABOUT TIME
MANAGEMENT

Let us start with some truths about time and time management that our gurus offer.

The first thing to know about time management is that you cannot manage time itself. Time exists or perhaps better passes in spite of what you do or don't do. Time itself is unmanageable. Time is an artificial concept, culturally created. Twenty-four hours per day, seven days per week, 365 days per year are concepts that exist only because people created them.

You can't find the time. You have to "manage" the time you have. As Rita Emmett, author *of Manage Your Time to Reduce Your Stress* says, you are not going to walk along a beach someday and find a bucket of extra time like a bucket of sand.

(Emmett 2009, p. 4)

You can't "SAVE" time. You can't put aside an hour or so today so that you will have more time to get things done tomorrow.

You can't do anything in your "FREE" time because there isn't any. You may have some leisure time, if you are lucky, but you will never have "FREE" time. All time has value.

(Griessman 1994, pp. ix-1)

You have all the time there is. If you live to 100, you have 52,596,000 minutes, the same as any other person who might live to be 100—no more and no less. [Do the math yourself; just don't forget leap years.]

If you are not getting as much done as someone else, it isn't because you don't have enough time. It is because you are not doing as good a job managing the time you have. The one thing you have in common with people you know or have heard of who are wealthy, powerful and famous is 24 hours each day. As Eugene Griessman says, "the difference between being successful and not being successful depends upon how you use your daily ratio of 24 hours."

(Griessman 1994, pp. ix-1)

Brian Tracy says, "Time management is really life management, personal management. It is really taking control of the sequence of events... what you do next." He notes that all of us, most of the time have the right to choose the task that we will do next and our ability and willingness to exercise that right is the key determinant of our success in life and at work.

(Tracy Eat *That Frog* 2007, p. 23)

Rita Emmett says you should "picture a continuum—a line with 'burned out' at one end and 'unlit' at the other." If you are at the burned out end, you have too much to do and the stress will eventually destroy you. However, it is also not good to be at the unlit end. If you are unlit, you have no motivation, no reason to get up in the morning. You end up bored most of the time. Ultimately, living without purpose will destroy you. The purpose of time management is to find the right spot for you along that continuum from unlit to burned out.

(Emmett 2009, pp. 38-39)

In short, our gurus tell us that time management is not about finding a way to get more stuff done. Time management is about finding a way to get MORE OF THE THINGS THAT REALLY MATTER done. In short, "Time Management" is really the wrong term for what we will be discussing in this book. We are really discussing "YOU" management or "WHAT YOU DO" management or, perhaps, "TIME USE MANAGEMENT."

MISCONCEPTIONS ABOUT TIME MANAGEMENT

Most people would probably agree that we would all be happier and more productive if we did a better job in managing our time. We may even know some of the things we should be doing to reduce stress and get more done like making a To-Do list, setting some personal and life goals, getting better organized, and so on. Still, most of us don't do a very good job in managing our time. Why is that? The truth is many people have some misconceptions about time management.

In his book *The Time Trap,* Alex Mackenzie, discusses some of the misconceptions about time management he hears most frequently. Do any of these apply to you?

"Time management is for people who are having trouble. I'm doing well at my job, so I must be managing my time just fine."

Mackenzie says that may be true, but you may be doing well not because of, but in spite of your time management practices. It is very likely that you could be a lot more successful if you just applied a few simple time management techniques.

"I work better under pressure; time management would take away that edge."

Mackenzie doubts it. He says you are just offering a subconscious rationale for procrastinating. In reality, you may be getting a reward for doing everything at the last minute. You look like a hero for getting the job done just in time.

The truth, says Mackenzie, is that people who put off things to the last minute hardly ever produce superior results since typically they don't plan and consequently, they leave no time to correct mistakes, locate missing information, or incorporate better ideas that might come to them too late to be included. By not managing your time, you deny yourself the opportunity to do outstanding work.

"I use an appointment calendar and a To-Do list. Isn't that enough?"

That's good, says Mackenzie, but the problem is most people don't use their calendar and To-Do list in the best way. They fill their To-Do list and calendar with one thing after another without regard to priority. A too full, non-prioritized To-Do List usually does more harm than good.

"Time management takes all the fun out of life."

So, says Mackenzie, you think constant stress, forgetting appointments, missing deadlines, and working until midnight are fun. He thinks you must have a strange idea of fun. Wouldn't it be more fun to reduce your stress, accomplish more and gain the equivalent of two extra hours every day? That's possible, says Mackenzie, if just practice a few simple time management techniques.

"Time management will take away my freedom- I'm a spontaneous sort of person."

Wrong, says Mackenzie, true freedom comes through discipline. Imagine, he says, that you suddenly had the opportunity to take a trip with your best friend to some place you had always wanted to visit. Suppose you were lucky enough to be able take that trip at a huge discount or even for free. Suppose you were so organized and up-to-date with your work that you could go. That's true freedom.

"Time management might be good for some kinds of work, but my job is very creative. I can't be tied to a routine."

You misunderstand time management, says Mackenzie. When you manage your time effectively, you are actually freeing up time to be creative. You are getting rid of the worry, tension, and tedious detail that stand in the way of creativity.

"The stuff they teach you in time management is a lot of work. I don't have time to do all that."

On the other hand, says Mackenzie, you have the time to waste hours in unproductive work. Mackenzie admits that his time management techniques take some work, but the few minutes it takes to do them can save you hours. You don't have time to do time management. Wrong, you don't have time not to. Mackenzie tells a story about a man struggling to cut down enough trees to build a fence that illustrates his point. An old farmer came by, watched for a while, then quietly said,

"Saw's kinda dull, isn't it?"

"I reckon," said the fence builder.

"Hadn't ya better sharpen it?"

"Maybe later. I can't stop now-I got all these trees to cut down."

Take Mackenzie's advice. Sharpen your time management saw. You'll be glad you did.

(Mackenzie 1997, pp. 11-12)

PERSONAL HINDRANCES

Finally, say Sandra Felton and Marsha Sims, authors of *Organizing Your Day*, you may find getting started with time management difficult for some very personal reasons.

YOU'RE NOT AN ORGANIZED PERSON:

You may be the smartest person in the world when it comes to your job or other aspects of your life, but you still may have a problem getting organized, setting priorities, making decisions, and so on. If that's you, then you really do need the advice of our gurus. The tips from our gurus we provide in the rest of this book may not make you a time management superstar, but they will help you if time management and getting organized is just not your thing. We are sure of that.

YOU ARE EASILY DISTRACTED:

You may have more trouble that other people staying focused. You find it hard to stick to one thing for very long. Well, our gurus have some good tips for how to avoid distractions that we will share later in this book.

YOU THINK YOU CAN'T MANAGE YOUR TIME:

Maybe you have read some time management books before or even taken some classes on time management. You tried some of the things you learned, but they just didn't seem to work for you. If that's you, take heart. This time we are going to give you a lot of different tools and techniques for managing your time from some of the smartest people around when it comes to getting organized and getting things done. Plus, we are going to give you a simple four-step process to follow.

YOU JUST MAY NOT BE NATURALLY FAST:

We all live our lives at a different pace. Some people are racing rabbits, some are methodical turtles. There is nothing wrong with that. After all, in the story of the turtle and the hare, who won the race?

YOU MAY NEED A CHECKUP:

If you are not getting everything done that you want to do and feel you should do, maybe there is a medical reason. If you have a low-grade infection or anemic or have some other yet undiagnosed medical problem, even a minor one, it may be standing in your way of getting things done. If you seem to be just dragging through life, you may need to check with a doctor. That's good advice even if you weren't planning to take a stab at time management right now. If something just doesn't feel right, get it checked out. Get it fixed. Time management can wait.

YOU'RE A CARETAKER:

There is nothing wrong with being a caretaker, caring about others, having a "helper" mentality. We certainly all need a caretaker at some point in our lives and are lucky to have them. However, you can take caretaking too far. The best caretakers take care to make sure they are teaching the people they are helping to take care of themselves eventually. The best caretakers want to work themselves out of a job. Our gurus offer some good advice about that in the section of this book on delegation.

YOU'RE JUST OVERWHELMED:

You look around and all you can see is one seemingly impossible task after another. You just don't know where to start, so you can't get started. Well, the gurus have some helpful hints for how to get un-overwhelmed. We cover those tips in the section on procrastination.

(Above from Felton and Sims 2009, pp 26-28)

Well, if any of these personal hindrances apply to you or Mackenzie's "tough love" has convinced you more than ever that you need to get busy sharpening your time management saw, then this book is for you, so let' get started. Here's how we plan to tackle the topic.

FOUR STEPS TO TIME MANAGEMENT

We will divide the rest of the book into four steps:

STEP ONE: SET YOUR PERSONAL GOALS AND PRIORITIES

We said earlier that the purpose of time management was not just to help you get MORE THINGS DONE but to help you get MORE OF THE IMPORTANT THINGS DONE. In Step 1, we will outline the steps our gurus' say you need to take to decide what is truly important to you. You will do that by setting some goals for your personal and professional future so that you can focus on what is important.

We cover Step 1 in Chapter Two—Set Your Personal Goals and Priorities.

STEP TWO: FIND YOUR TIME WASTERS

In this step, we share our gurus' advice on how to keep and analyze some simple time logs to find out how you are currently spending your time and what might be getting in your way when it comes to getting more of the important things done.

We cover Step 2 in Chapter Three—Identify Your Time Wasters.

STEP THREE: DEPLOY TIME MANAGEMENT TOOLS AND TECHNIQUES

In Step 3, we will present a number of simple time management tools and techniques that the gurus say many people have found useful to help them reduce or eliminate their time wasters.

We cover Step 3 in Chapter 4—Deploy Time Management Tools and Techniques.

STEP FOUR: GET AND STAY ORGANIZED

Finally, we will show you how to use a technique called the "5S" process that our gurus recommend as a great way to get organized.

We cover Step 4 in Chapter 5: Get and Stay Organized.

We will begin by helping you sort out your goals and priorities. But first, let's review some KEY IDEAS from this chapter.

KEY IDEAS

- You can't find the time. You already have all the time there is. If you are not getting as much done as someone else, it isn't because you don't have enough time. It is because you are not doing as good a job managing the time you have.

- Time management is really all about taking control of the sequence of events in your life. You manage time by taking control over what you do next and next and next.

- The purpose of time management is NOT to get MORE THINGS DONE but to get MORE OF THE IMPORTANT THINGS DONE.

- There are four steps to time management
  - o Determine life goals
  - o Identify your time wasters
  - o Eliminate or reduce your time wasters
  - o Get and stay organized.

22....Joseph H. Boyett & Jimmie T. Boyett

CHAPTER TWO--SET YOUR PERSONAL GOALS AND PRIORITIES

It is unfortunate but true that most of us spend 80% of our hours each day doing things that don't really matter and only 20% of our valuable time working on important things. Time management will help you reverse those numbers. You may not be able to eliminate spending time on relatively unimportant things, but you should try to allow those time wasters to take up 20% or less of your time so you can focus 80% or more of your time on those things that will help you achieve your goals. Of course, to do that, you have to understand your personal and professional goals. That's what Step 1 involves.

Note: Even if you think you have some well thought out goals and objectives for your career and life, we still suggest you work through this step if nothing more than to confirm that what you thought was important the last time you thought about your goals still is.

WHAT ARE YOUR BIG PICTURE GOALS?

Julie Morgenstern, author of *Time Management from the Inside Out*, says you should begin by thinking about the BIG PICTURE. What do you want to accomplish when it comes to the aspects of your life that are most important such as:

Your Health: Maybe your goal is to lose weight or gain body strength.

Your Intellectual Development: Maybe you want to go back to school or take a course on a topic that interests you just for fun.

Your Social Life: Maybe you want to spend more time with your friends or finally meet Mr. /Ms. Right.

Your Family: Maybe you want to spend more time with your children.

Your Work: Maybe you want to get a promotion or own a business one day.

Your Finances: Maybe you want to get out of debt or buy a house.

Your Community: Maybe you want to find time to volunteer.

Your Spiritual Well-Being: Maybe you want to find ways to become a kinder, gentler and more caring person.

Note: Not only should you think about your goals in all of these BIG PICTURE categories, but also you should think about how you want to find balance between them. How can you expand your social life without hurting your relationships with your family? How can you advance your career without being mean or selfish or hurting others?

Morgenstern 2004, pp. 165-169

WHY ARE BIG PICTURE GOALS IMPORTANT?

Donald Wetmore, author of *The Productivity Handbook* reminds us that we pay a big price when we neglect our

BIG GOALS or the balance between them. He notes that:

- 75% of people who die each year in the U.S. die prematurely because they did not take adequate care of their health
- 50% of marriages end in divorce usually because of a lack of communication. That's not surprising given that the average working person spends less than two minutes in meaningful communication with their spouse or significant other each day and only thirty seconds with their children.
- The average American spends about 50% of their waking hours just making a living. The key difference between those who amass riches and those who don't is how the rich manage their time.
- Half of all human knowledge was unknown twenty years ago. Regardless of your occupation, if you don't' continue to learn, your skills will be obsolete not in decades but in years.

(Wetmore 2005 pp. 6-16)

Edward Hallowell, author of *Crazy Busy*, says we should all think of ourselves as having a time account—the time we have left before we die. How much longer do you think you might live? Let's say, you think you can make it to 100. Break that down in minutes. How many minutes are there before you reach 100? That's your time account. How well are you using the minutes in your time account? How are you using your time? Are you investing the minutes you have left in those things that really matter to you? Do a little time accounting as you think about your big goals for your life?

(Hallowell 2006, pp. 145-150)

SOME GOAL EXERCISES TO TRY

Figuring out what is important isn't easy. Don't be surprised if completing this step in your journey to better time management turns out to be difficult. As Warren Bennis, who has written extensively on leadership and goal setting, once wrote, "if knowing yourself and being yourself were as easy to do as to talk about, there wouldn't be nearly as many people walking around in borrowed postures, spouting secondhand ideas, trying desperately to fit in rather than to stand out." (Quoted in Joseph Boyett & Jimmie Boyett, *The Guru Guide: The Best Ideas of the Top Management Thinkers*. New York: John Wiley, 1998, p. 29) Good or not, it seems that most of us just muddle through life, never setting a specific course. Reluctant to pick a course, we trust our lives more to happenstance than our own judgment. Don't let that be you. Set your own course. How? Try these exercises.

Dave Allen, author of *Getting Things Done,* says as you do these goals exercises, keep in mind that you are going to have various levels of goals for different time periods. He uses an aerospace analogy in talking about levels of goals. He says you should think of your various levels of goals this way:

50,000+feet: These are your lifetime goals. What do you want to accomplish during the time you have left on earth? Brian Tracy, author of *Time Power*, says you should really dream big when you are thinking about these lifetime goals. Tracy says you should imagine that you have no limitations and put all mental roadblocks and excuses aside. You will only achieve your full potential if you have goals that are truly exciting and challenging toward which you can work enthusiastically every day.

(Tracy *Time Power* 2007, pp 28-32)

40,000 feet: This is your three-to-five year vision for yourself. Think about your career, trends in your organization or society, life-transitions you will go through, your family and financial goals and commitments, all the things that are likely to occur or you want to occur over the next three-to-five years.

30,000 feet: These are your goals for the next one to two years. These are the personal or professional goals you have for the next couple of years that will move you forward toward achieving your three-to-five year vision and ultimately your lifetime goals.

20,000 feet: These are your areas of responsibility. These are responsibilities you have toward your job/career such as planning, supporting others, doing research, providing customer service, managing assets and so on. They also include your personal responsibilities with regard to your health, your family, your finances, and so on.

10,000 feet: Current projects. These are the things you need to do or want to accomplish over the next few days or weeks to meet your responsibilities and move toward your multi-year and lifetime goals.

Runway: Current actions. These are the things on your daily To-Do list.

28….Joseph H. Boyett & Jimmie T. Boyett

(Allen 2001, pp. 51-53)

We will show you how to prepare a daily To-Do list later. For now, try these goal exercises.

NOTE: We hope you will do at least some of the Goals Exercises that follow. We know you would like to finish this book as soon as possible. After all, you are pressed for time. However, we hope you will stop reading this book for a day, or longer, to do one or more of these exercises. You will get much more out of the remainder of this book if you do.

GOALS EXERCISE #1: PATTERN SEARCH

Find a quiet, safe, reflective environment where you can get away from day-to-day activities and do some serious reflection-- a church, garden, mountain top, under an oak tree in your backyard, the seashore, a park, or in your most comfortable chair surrounded by plants and soothing music. Leave the cell phone behind.

Reflect on your early childhood and how it shaped your development. Look for behaviors, motivations, and values that your parents taught you. Think about all of the following:

Family composition:

What was your birth position, family rules, expectations, and economic status? What feelings do you have about your family? What traditions did you have? Think about personal characteristics you feel are genetic or inherited.

Gender significance:

Being male or female certainly influences the way we think and what we believe is possible. To grasp the significance of gender, write down 10 ways your life would be different if you were a member of the opposite sex.

Geographic influences:

Where were you born? Even different regions within a country have diverse cultures and lifestyles. Ask people who were born in a different region or country about the customs, pastimes, and the aspects they consider unique about growing up in that area.

Cultural background:

For some people, cultural identity is a key to understanding who they are, while others have little awareness of their heritage. What would you describe as your culture? How significant has this been in shaping your life? How has your culture woven the fabric of your purpose as a person?

Generational influences:

Events that occur during the particular period of time in which people are born shape their lives and give identity to their generation. One need only to talk to a baby boomer to understand the importance of generational influences, such as television or computers. Certain influences are so pervasive that they touch the majority of people's lives, such as the changing role of women in the workplace and in the family, the advent of the global marketplace, or the demographic changes that are taking place in America.

How have these and other experiences of your generation affected your beliefs, standards, expectations?

Write down your answers to these questions. What do they tell you about what you value and who you are? What BIG GOALS do your answers suggest for your life?

FAMILY COMPOSITION

Questions	My Answers
Where were you in the birth order?	
What were your family rules, expectations, and economic status?	
What feelings do you have about your family?	
What traditions do you have in your family?	
What personal characteristics do you have that you feel are genetic or inherited?	

GENDER SIGNIFICANCE

	Ways My Life Would Be Different
1.	
2.	
3.	
4.	
5.	
6.	
7.	
8.	
9.	
10.	

GEOGRAPHICAL and CULTURAL INFLUENCES

What customs, pastimes, or other factors are unique to the area where you grew up? List the ways they shaped your life.
1.
2.
3.
4.
5.
6.
7.
8.
9.
10.

GENERATIONAL INFLUENCES

What customs, pastimes, or other factors are unique to your generation shaped your life?
1.
2.
3.
4.
5.
6.
7.
8.
9.
10.

GOALS EXERCISE # 2: YOUR LIFE TIMELINE

Draw a timeline of your life and list your major activities and jobs in chronological order. For each point along the timeline, list the skills and talents that you exhibited as you moved through life. Group these skills by category-people-related, technical, intellectual, communication, and so on. What were your greatest strengths? Which skills and talents did you enjoy using? In what areas did you excel? What came easy to you? What have you learned? What is the deeper meaning behind your experiences? What inspired you and why?

1970 1975 1980 1985 1990 1995 2000 2005 2010

------|------|------|------|-------|------|------|------|------|------

Write down your answers to these questions. What do they tell you about what you value and who you are? What BIG GOALS do your answers suggest for your life?

Date(s)	Event (What I liked. What made it special. What talents I used.)	Big Goal/Values

GOALS EXERCISE # 3: MOMENTS OF DECISION

Think of moments in your life when you made significant decisions that may not have seemed most logical or expedient at the time but just "felt right."

Write down your answers to these questions. What do they tell you about what you value and who you are? What BIG GOALS do your answers suggest for your life?

Area	What My Decision Tells Me About My Big Picture Goals
Health	
Intellectual Development	
Social Life	
Family	
Work	
Finances	
Community	
Spiritual Well-Being	

GOALS EXERCISE #4: THE LOTTERY WINNER

Ask yourself, "What would I do even if I didn't get paid for it? What do I dream about doing? What is my passion? What would I do if I won the lottery, had only six months to live, or could live in good health for 100 years?" And yes, your answer can be to play golf, travel, or shop 'till you drop.

Area	A Big Picture Goal I Would Have If I Won the Lottery
Health	
Intellectual Development	
Social Life	
Family	
Work	
Finances	
Community	
Spiritual Well-Being	

(Goals exercises 1-4 were suggested by Juana Bordas, "Power and Passion: Finding Personal Purpose," in *Reflections on Leadership*, Lary C. Spears, Ed., New York: John Wiley & Sons, 1995, pp. 184-192.)

GOALS EXERCISE #5: WRITE YOUR BIOGRAPHY

Brian Tracy suggested this one. Tracy says you should try to project yourself forward to the end of your life and imagine you were writing your own biography. What would you want said about your life and accomplishments in your biography? How do you want people to remember you?

(Tracy *Time Power* 2007, pp. 32-39)

Tracy says writing your own life story and/or your obituary will help you take a "long-term perspective" which is just what you must do if you really want to get at what is truly important to you.

GOALS EXERCISE #5: THE THINGS YOU LOVE TO DO

This one is also from Tracy. It is like the Life Timeline Exercise above. Tracy says think about what things you have done in your life that gave you the greatest sense of accomplishment or satisfaction. What one thing would you do all day long if you could? That's a good indicator, says Tracy, of not only what is important to you, but also what you are actually likely to perform the best.

Tracy says that the things you love to do are usually the things that you are ideally suited to do. It makes sense then to organize your life around those tasks and activities since they are the things that you are most likely to have the natural talents and abilities to perform well. They are the key to your peak performance and highest achievement.

(Tracy *Time Power* 2007, pp. 32-39)

GOALS EXERCISE #6: KEEP A "JOY JOURNAL"

Julie Morgenstern makes a similar argument. She says you should keep an electronic or paper "Joy Journal." Each day, pay attention to what delights you as you go through each day. Whenever you find yourself doing something that you enjoy, Morgenstern says you should write it down in your Joy Journal. She recommends that you keep your Joy Journal for a month. Then, review it to see if you can detect any patterns. What gave you JOY! Use what you learn from reviewing your Joy Journal to create goals that will allow you to do as many of the things that give you JOY everyday of your life.

(Morgenstern 2004, pp. 165-169)

GOALS EXERCISE #7: LOOK INTO AN IMAGINARY CRYSTAL BALL

Alternatively—or in addition—Morgenstern says imagine that ten years from now you will have gotten everything you want out of life. Imagine that you have a magic Crystal Ball that will show you what your life will be like then. What would your crystal ball reveal about your life—a life in which you have gotten everything you want?

(Morgenstern 2004, pp. 165-169)

WRITE YOUR SMART GOALS

Now that you have spent at least a day working through some of the goals exercises—You did that, didn't you?—it's time to write your goals.

Before you do, Rita Emmett warns that just any type of goals won't do. She says many people decide upon a goal like losing weight or resolving a conflict with someone who used to be their friend or starting a new business. Then, a year later or a few months later, nothing is different, nothing has happened. It is as if they never had a goal at all. Emmett says there are three problems most people have with setting personal and professional goals. First, they set a goal that is unrealistic because important actions that would be required for them to achieve the goal are out of their control. Let's suppose you say to yourself that this year, you are going to mend the fences with your old friend. You are going to get back the relationship you had before the two of you had that disagreement that is keeping you apart. Emmett says, fine. However, keep in mind that your former friend has a lot of control over whether you are able to achieve your goal. If she doesn't want to restore the friendship, then it is not going to happen. Better to set a goal to invite your former friend to lunch or out for dinner. She might turn you down. You can't control whether she accepts your invitation. You can control issuing the invitation. You control that positive goal

Second says, Emmett, people often make the mistake of setting vague goals with no time limit. If your goal is to start a business--someday--or lose some weight—sometime--you don't really have a goal. You have a wish. Wishing doesn't get you there. A Goal would be to write a business plan by August 1st or start weight loss classes by May 15th.

Finally, Emmett says people make the mistake of setting an unmeasurable goal. Consequently, they have no way of ever determining whether they achieved their goal. You want to start a successful business. Good, but how will you measure success. Is it profits, number of customers, revenues? What is your measure of success?

(Emmett 2009, pp. 70-71)

Our gurus say if you want to have goals that work, you need to convert what you have learned from the goals exercises into several SMART goals.

A goal is SMART if it is:

S = Specific—the goal clearly specifies what you want to accomplish with a timeframe for completion. Begin with "I" and use action verbs... create, design, develop, implement, obtain, produce, etc. Example: I will obtain my Bachelor's degree in xxx by dd/mm/yy.

M = Measurable: How will you know when you have obtained your goal? For example, you could measure the achievement of the goal to obtain a degree by presenting the diploma.

A = Achievable: The goal may be a "stretch" but it must be feasible. Is it reasonable to expect that you could achieve this goal with the resources you have at your disposal? If not, then you may need an intermediate goal. For example, if you don't currently have the money to pay tuition to start work on your college degree, you may need to set a goal to save a certain amount a month to build a tuition fund.

R = Relevant: The goal should help to improve one or more of the BIG PICTURE areas of your life we discussed earlier: Your health, intellectual development, social life, family, work, finances, community, and spiritual well-being.

T =Time-bound: The Goal should identify a definite target date for completion and/or frequencies for specific action steps that are important for achieving the goal. Incorporate specific dates, calendar milestones, or timeframes that are relative to the achievement of another result (i.e., dependencies and linkages to other projects). For example, the goal to obtain a Bachelor's degree by June 20xx might include as an intermediate sub-goal "Begin taking courses toward my degree by September 20, xxxx."

Here are some examples of personal SMART goals to get you started:

- I am weighing xxx lbs., eating a salad every day and exercising four times a week by Dec 20, xxxx.

- I am reading one book every month, twelve books a year by June 20, xxxx.

- I am moving into my brand new three-bedroom apartment by July 20, xxxx. I have views of both a river and a park and have private parking. The shops are only a 5-minute walk away.

- I have set up a bank account for my new business, already taken 2000 dollars in sales and generated 500 dollars profit all by October 20, xxxx.

- I play with my children every day and reading them a nighttime story every evening by January 20, xxxx.

(Prentice 2005, 91-92 suggests SMART goals as do most of our other gurus)

Notice that we wrote these goals in the present tense. Brian Tracy, author of *Time Power*, says that's important because positive, present-tense goals program your subconscious and build faith and conviction that your goal is realizable. And, he says, you should repeat your goal to yourself often because, "the more often you read and repeat your goal, the deeper you program it into your mind, and the sooner you begin to become absolutely convinced that you will attain this goal, exactly when the timing is right for you."

(Tracy *Time Power* 2007, pp. 28-32)

WRITE THREE SMART GOALS

Your task in this chapter is to write THREE SMART goals in at least some of these areas based upon what you learned from completing one or more of the goals exercises.

	Smart Goal Specific, Measurable, Achievable, Relevant, Time-bound	S	M	A	R	T
#1						
#2						
#3						

KEY IDEAS

- You can't begin to effectively manage your time until you know your Big Picture Goals—what you want to accomplish in your personal and professional life.

- Your Big Picture Goals should relate to one or more of the following aspects of your life: your health, your intellectual development, your social life, your work, your finances, your community, and/or your spiritual well-being.

- You should have at least three WRITTEN SMART GOALS. Smart Goals are:

    o Specific

    o Measurable

    o Achievable

    o Relevant

    o Time-bound

42….Joseph H. Boyett & Jimmie T. Boyett

CHAPTER THREE: Identify Your Time Wasters

You now have defined at least three SMART goals to pursue. Your next task is to find out what is standing in your way of achieving your goals, the TIME WASTERS. Once you know the TIME WASTERS that are costing you the most time, you can then start to use the time management tools and techniques we cover in the next chapter to get rid of as many as possible.

BEGIN KEEPING A TIME LOG

You need to keep a Time Log to begin finding your time wasters.

A Time Log is just a simple record of how you spend your time. Alec Mackenzie, author of *The Time Trap* recommends that you keep your time log for a minimum of three days, a week is even better. Mackenzie recommends that you set up a log with five columns: Time Started, Activity, Duration, Priority, and Comments.

TIME STARTED	ACTIVITY	DURATION	PRIORITY	COMMENTS
7:45	Linda told me about a movie she saw	20 min	4	
8:10	Cleaned my desk	35 min	2	Should do this at the end of the day
8:45	Meeting with Tracy about report	15 min	1	

44....Joseph H. Boyett & Jimmie T. Boyett

(Mackenzie 1997, 48-49)

Cultivate your lilies and get rid of your leeches.
(Hallowell 2006, p. 163)

HOW TO KEEP YOUR TIME LOG

1. **Time Started**-Record the time each new activity started as the day progresses in the Time Started column. When you switch from one activity to another throughout the day, enter the time you switched.

2. **Description**-Enter a brief description of what you were doing (the activity) in the Activity column. Try to capture all interruptions. Write down why the interruption occurred, including as much detail about the interruption as you remember.

3. **Duration**-Make a note in the Duration column about how much time you spent on each item.

4. **Priority**-Set a priority for every single item and record it in the Priority column. The point is that at the end of the day you will look back and see what proportion of time you spent on high-priority work. Ask yourself how important is this activity in terms of helping you achieve one or more of the goals you identified in Step 1? Assign priorities as follows: (1) Important (Must do because it is critical to achieving one or more of my personal or professional goals), (2) Important (Should do because it might help me achieve my goals), (3) Routine (Could Do since it wouldn't distract from my achieving my goals), (4) Time Wasters (Why did I do this? —Not important to achieving my

goals or may prevent me from achieving my goals) You can do this at the end of the day.

5. **Comments**-In a "Comments" column, record your thoughts about what you can learn from each interruption or change of activity. How could you have made better use of your time? Try to jot down your comments as you go along since if you wait until the end of the day you may forget important details.

(Sources: Mackenzie 1997, 48-49; Luecke 2005, 20-21 recommends a similar log and priorities.)

Time management doesn't mean running around like a nut doing twenty things at once. True time management means actually spending as much of your time as you can doing those things you want to do rather than activities you don't care about. It involves clarifying your values, deciding what is important, and working to spend your time doing that. (Emmett 2009, p. 30)

FIND YOUR TIME WASTERS

Review your 3 to 5 days of time logs to identify your time wasters. TIME WASTERS come in a variety of guises. Some even pretend to be time savers, but aren't. Here are a few examples of the most notorious time wasters our gurus say many people encounter:

- *HAVING NO PLAN OR SCHEDULE:* Moving from one task to another with no plan or schedule or trying to perform difficult tasks at the wrong time of day when you are tired or distracted.

- *PROCRASTINATING:* Working on unimportant activities as a way of putting off what you don't want to do or find difficult

- *DELAYS OR DOWNTIME:* Doing nothing when you could be accomplishing something when you encounter an unexpected delay.

- *BEING INTERRUPTED:* Spending time with unexpected visitors, phone calls, email, text messages, etc. that don't help you achieve your personal or professional goals.

- *NOT DELEGATING:* Spending time on activities that you should have delegated to someone else.

- *NOT SAYING NO:* Spending time on activities that are not important to you just because you did not say NO.

- *MEANINGLESS MEETINGS:* Spending time in meetings you don't need to attend.

- *IMPROPERLY HANDLING MAIL/EMAIL:* Spending too much time handling mail or email.

- *NOT MANAGING PHONE CALLS*: Spending too much time on the phone.

- *NOT MANAGING INTERNET USAGE:* Spending too much time on the internet

- *NOT BEING ORGANIZED:* Spending too much time looking for paper files, computer files, addresses and other things you need to complete your work.

- *CORRECTION AND REWORK:* Spending time fixing work that was not performed correctly the first time.

- *WAITING:* Idle time when work stops because people, paper, machines or information needed to get the job done are not available.

- *UNNECESSARY MOTION:* Walking, reaching, bending and so on caused by ineffective job process and/or poor office design.

- *OVERPROCESSING:* Effort expended on the performance of a task that provides something the customer for the task doesn't want or need.

- *EQUIPMENT DOWNTIME:* Breakdowns and/or slowness because of poor equipment maintenance or usage planning.

- *EXCESS STORAGE:* Purchase and storage of excess supplies, tools, equipment, books, files and so on that aren't needed or could easily be replaced when needed.

- *INSPECTION:* Checking and error correction because work is not performed correctly the first time.

(Sources: Mackenzie 1997, 247-268 and Fabrizio and Tapping 2006, pp. 5-8)

MORE TIME WASTERS

Eugene Griessman, author of *Time Tactics of Very Successful People*, adds three additional time wasters that might show up in your time log.

Doing something that is not worth doing: If you spend time on things that aren't worth doing, you are diverting time and energy from things worth doing. You think you are accomplishing something, but you really aren't. Worse, unnecessary tasks may take on a life of their own—you do it just because you always have. And, the unnecessary task may generate what Griessman calls "not worth doing *babies*," sub-tasks that you do just because you are doing the "daddy" necessary task. Look for these unnecessary "daddy" and "baby" tasks in your time log.

Quitting too soon: Check your time log for tasks that went uncompleted. Maybe you got 90% done and just quit, perhaps because you got bored or you just didn't feel like continuing. Griessman says when you quit too soon you waste all of the time you have already devoted to the task.

Failing to cut your losses: This is the opposite of "quitting too soon." In this case, you stubbornly persist with a task long past the time you should have given up on it. Griessman says when you begin to suspect that something is no longer worth pursuing, ask yourself questions such as the following and answer honestly:

- Can you get additional information or advice from and expert who might help you decide if it is time to quit?

- Have you reached the "walkaway position"?

- Have you reached an impenetrable barrier, something you can't overcome?

- Will further engagement result in major losses?

- Is the potential payoff worth the additional effort or cost to finish?

When you reach the point where you question the wisdom of proceeding, you need to decide when and whether it is best to just walk away and accept your losses. Maybe you have done all you can. Griessman says an important time management lesson is to accept that in many cases good enough is just that, good enough. Perfection may not be necessary. In fact, perfection may be undesirable. Griessman says, "The game is won by those who clear all the hurdles not those who clear most hurdles by an extra amount. There may be no advantage and a significant cost in trying to be 2% better. The best hurdlers clear all of the hurdles, just barely."

(Griessman 1994, pp. 86-96)

Rita Emmett says striving for excellence is important. Excellence is achievable. Just remember that few people ever truly achieve perfection. She says; think about something that you experienced, a party, wedding, vacation, and so on that you remember as just perfect. Then, think back on that event. Was it really so perfect? Chances are a lot of things didn't go exactly right. But you still considered the event a success, something you remember fondly.

(Emmett 2009, pp. 52-53)

KEY IDEAS

- Once you have identified your personal and professional Big Goals, you need to keep a time log for at least three days to a week to see how you are currently spending your time.

- You should record the time each activity starts, a description of each activity you engaged in during the day, the duration of the activity, its priority, and any comments on about the activity.

- Give each activity a priority such as: Important-Must Do, Important-Should Do, Routine-Could Do, or Time Waster-Not relevant to my goals.

- Analyze your time log to find time wasters such as:
    - Having no plan or schedule;
    - Procrastinating;
    - Not making the most of delays or downtime;
    - Being interrupted;
    - Not delegating;
    - Not saying NO;
    - Meaningless meetings;
    - Not managing mail, email, phone calls or internet usage;
    - Not being organized;
    - Correction and rework;
    - Waiting;
    - Unnecessary motion;
    - Overprocessing;
    - Equipment downtime;

- o Excess storage;
- o Inspection;
- o Doing something not worth doing;
- o Quitting too soon; or
- o Failing to cut your losses.

52....Joseph H. Boyett & Jimmie T. Boyett

CHAPTER FOUR: DEPLOY TIME MANAGEMENT TOOLS AND TECHNIQUES

You identified your personal and professional goals in step one. You identified your personal time wasters in step two. Now it is time to find time management tools and techniques to help you stop wasting time on unimportant things so that you can focus the time you have on activities that will help you achieve your goals.

We listed examples of the most notorious time wasters in the last chapter. In this chapter, we discuss some of the tools, tips and techniques many people have found useful in reducing the time they spend on some of the biggest time wasters most people encounter.

- **Having No Plan or Schedule:** Moving from one task to another with no plan or schedule or trying to perform difficult tasks at the wrong time of day when you are tired or distracted.

- **Procrastinating:** Working on unimportant activities as a way of putting off what you don't want to do or find difficult.

- **Not Making the Most of Delays or Downtime:** Doing nothing when you could be accomplishing something when you are unexpectedly delayed.

- **Being Interrupted:** Spending time with unexpected visitors, phone calls, email, text messages, etc. that don't help you achieve your personal or professional goals.

- **Not Delegating:** Spending time on activities that you should have delegated to someone else.

- **Not Saying NO**: Spending time on activities that are not important to you just because you did not say NO.

- **Meaningless Meetings:** Spending time in meetings you don't need to attend.

- **Improperly Handling Physical Mail or Email:** Spending too much time handling mail or email.

- **Not Being Organized:** Spending too much time looking for paper files, computer files, addresses and other things you need to complete your work. [We discuss this time waster in Chapter 5.]

TOOL #1: PREPARE A DAILY TO-DO LIST

We start our discussion of time management tools and techniques with the most popular tool of all—the To-Do list. If you employ just one time management tool and technique, this is the one provided, of course, that you use it correctly. Jan Yager says, "The number one reason people have trouble managing their time is that they try to do too much at once." He says a third of people try to do so many different things in the same day or at the same time that they end up getting little, if anything at all done. They are STARTERS but seldom FINISHERS. The reason they finish so little, says Yager, is that if they have a To-Do list at all, it isn't prioritized and they start work on a second item on the list before finishing the first or they just skip around from one item to another.

(Yager 1999, pp. 14-15)

As the name suggests, a To-Do list is a list of things you need to do today.

A To-Do List is neither **a random list of activities unrelated to your personal and professional goals (See Step One)** nor **a stack of jotted notes of reminders on bits of paper.**

A To-Do List **IS** a written plan for your day consisting of a list of activities where each activity:

- Is related to achieving one or more of your personal or professional SMART goals

- Has a designated A-B-C priority such as:

    o A=Crucial

    o B=Important

    o C=Little Value

    o *=A Quick item that can be done in less than 5 minutes.

- Includes an estimate of how long the activity/task will take.

Activity	Priority	Time to Complete

MAKE YOUR TO-DO LIST EFFECTIVE

Make an actual To Do List. Do not rely on scraps of paper or paper/electronic Post-it notes. Be sure your list covers the BIG PICTURE areas of your life (See Step One), not just work goals. Your BIG PICTURE areas include SMART goals for your work, plus goals for the following:

- Your Health.

- Your Intellectual Development.

- Your Social Life.

- Your Family.

- Your Finances.

- Your Community.

- Your Spiritual Well-Being.

Elaine St. James, author of *Simplify Your Work Life*, says that on your long-term To-Do list you should "block off every single weekend for the next six months" to spend time with your family, on personal non-work-related projects and/or to enjoy life. Your goal should be to manage your time in such a way that you can completely fulfill your responsibilities on the job without having to work on weekends.

(St. James 2001, pp. 17-18)

Julie Morgenstern says in preparing your To-Do list for the next day the most important thing to get on the list is the one task you will be thrilled to accomplish the next day if you got nothing else done. Schedule to do that task during the first hour of the day. During that hour turn off email, voice mail, don't get involved in a conversation with someone—do nothing that first hour, but concentrate on the one critical task you have set for yourself for that day. [Note: Some gurus disagree with Morgenstern. See our discussion of Morning Birds and Night Owls and scheduling when to perform a task later in this section.]

(Morgenstern 2004, p. 98)

You do not have to list an activity for each of your BIG PICTURE areas every day, but you should make sure that over the course of a week or a month, you are addressing all of these areas that you have established as priorities.

Supplement your daily To-Do List with an electronic or paper calendar where you record important commitments, target dates, and so on. Consult this calendar, looking ahead several days or weeks as you think about items for your daily To-Do List.

Consider having multiple To-Do lists: daily, short-term (this week), medium-term (this month/quarter), long-term (this year). Consult your short, medium and long-term lists as you prepare each daily list. Brian Tracy recommends that you keep four different lists:

- A Master List of everything you think of that you want to do in the future

- A Monthly List of everything that you want to do the next month

- A Weekly List of everything you want to do next week.

- A Daily List of everything you need to accomplish the next day.

(Tracy Eat *That Frog* 2007, pp. 16-17)

Tracy recommends that you set up what he calls a "45-file system." Get a box that will hold 45 hanging files.

- Label files 1 thru 31 for the days of the month

- Label the next 12 files for the months of the year

- Label the final two files for the next two years.

When you have an appointment or something to do put a note and accompanying information about the action in the day, month or year file where it belongs.

On the first day of each month, take out the file containing information on actions required that month and sort the actions into the daily files 1 thru 31. Each day, take out that day's file and use the information in planning your daily To-Do list.

(Tracy *Time Power* 2007, pp. 63-64)

Do not let your To-Do list get too large. Move lower priority items you know you will not have time to address on a given day onto a separate "Holding list." Consult that list for items to move onto your daily list when you are preparing each day's list.

Set priorities for each item on your To-Do list. Brian Tracy recommends an ABCDE method of setting priorities where A=Must Do, B=Should Do, C=Nice to Do, D=Delegate, and E= Eliminate.

(Tracy *Time Power* 2007, pp. 85-86)

Michelle Tullier suggest this method of setting priorities based upon ideas from Stephen Covey's book *The Seven Habits of Highly Effective People*:

- Urgent and important—i.e. Putting out fires
- Not urgent but important—Activities that will allow us to achieve our goals, build relationships and avoid crises
- Urgent but not important—Interruptions about matters that are not truly important—time wasters

- Not urgent and not important—Busywork we engage in that might make us feel like we are getting things done when we are really just avoiding dealing with important things that we find difficult or unpleasant.

(Tullier 2000, p. 62)

Eugene Griessman suggests that you establish just three priorities: A=High, B=Medium and C=Low based upon your answers to the following questions:

- Will it help me reach some important goal in my life?

- Does it have a deadline-a real deadline, like April 15?

- Is it an *order* from someone I can't ignore, like a supervisor or a commanding officer?

- Does it involve doing something important for my work or business?

- Will doing it advance my career, or conversely, will *not* doing / it hinder my career?

- Will it make me more knowledgeable or help me fulfill my potential?

- Will it require coordinated efforts with others? If so, can I get those people started on their parts of the project right away? Then can I turn my attention to something that doesn't require their input?

- Is it important to someone I really care about?

- Will it matter a year from now?

- Will it really matter if I don't do it?

60....Joseph H. Boyett & Jimmie T. Boyett

(Griessman 1994, p. 7)

Tracy says you should set "priorities" and "posteriorities." Posteriorities are things you do less of, later or stop doing. He says ask yourself these questions while setting priorities.

- What am I going to stop doing?
- What am I going to cut out, eliminate or delete?
- What am I doing today that, knowing what I now know, I would not have started doing if I had it to do over?"

He adds that whenever you add a new task, you should find a current task you can eliminate. Assume your dance card is always full. You need to defer, delay or delegate an existing task before you can take on something new. "Picking up something that you haven't done requires putting down something that you were already working on."

(Tracy *Time Power* 2007, pp. 84-85)

Break large tasks or complicated activities on your To-Do list down into smaller steps. Set weekly or monthly milestones (activities to be completed) for each major project. Set aside blocks of time each day on your To-Do list to work on these long-term projects. You may want to set aside specific blocks of time each day or week during which you can concentrate on tasks related to long-term projects with minimal distractions.

Use the "verb/noun" approach. Items on your To-Do list should be short and contain a verb and a noun such as:

1. Write memo.

2. Distribute Memo.

3. Call repairperson.

In estimating the time each item will take to complete, consider hidden time costs such as:

- Interruptions (We will discuss how to deal with the most common later in this book.)

- Travel time

- Unexpected delays

- Personal time—eating, breaks, restroom, etc.

- Set up and take down time

Steve Prentice says you should practice "crisis anticipation" when preparing your To-Do list. "The key to crisis anticipation is to think through, in advance, the different delays and setbacks that can possibly knock the project off schedule. Where could you have an obstacle or setback that would threaten the successful completion of the project? Once you have determined the worst possible thing that can happen, make sure that it doesn't happen. Address problems before they occur and take steps against them in advance."

(Prentice 2005, p. 128)

Never assume that things will go smoothly. Try to be prepared. Plan for what might go wrong and have a plan B. Donald Wetmore says when you actually think about the real number of hours you have available to get things done each day it is a lot less than you imagine. "Let's say you are scheduled to work 8 hours, exclusive of lunch, breaks and commuting. But you have a couple of meetings to attend. Subtract those and the time you need to prepare for them and you only have 6 hours left. But you know that someone or something will interrupt you during those 6 hours. Let's say interruptions usually eat up 2 hours. That leaves you with only 4 hours to get stuff on your to-do lists done. You have only half the time you thought you had."

(Wetmore 2005, pp. 21-31.)

Roberta Roesch, author of *Time Management for Busy People* says you should plan to have only six hours of productive work time out of every 8-hour workday.

(Roesch 1998, p. 12)

Assume that you will encounter unexpected delays or downtime such as waiting for an appointment, waiting for a meeting to start, sitting in traffic. Keep your To-Do list with you. Check your list for quick items you can complete or work on while you are waiting. Donald Wetmore says you should always have stuff with you to work on—pieces of a project, a professional journal/magazine to read, email to answer, a phone call to make—so you can turn downtime into productive time. Of course, it doesn't always have to be work. One of your SMART goals should be to take care of you. Downtime is the perfect time to do some YOU stuff—play a game, read an interesting book, listen to an audio book or lecture, work on an intriguing puzzle, just sit and think, or "just stop and smell a rose."

(Wetmore 2005, pp. 39-40)

Brian Tracy says when estimating how much time a task will take, make your best estimate and then ADD twenty percent. Then, he says, work as if it is absolutely necessary that you get the task done BEFORE your original best estimate.

(Tracy Eat *That Frog* 2007, p. 30)

Steve Prentice says you should reserve 15% of every day for what he calls "Opportunity Time." You purposely set that time aside each day for the unexpected. It might be time you have available to respond to a crisis. It is time you set aside to take advantage of an unexpected opportunity to advance your career or improve your personal life. It could be time you have available just for some reflection on your career and life or time just to unwind a little.

(Prentice 2005, pp. 73-74)

Divide your To-Do List into segments according to how you arrange your day such as "Before Work," "During Work," "After Work."

Don't try to multitask. When making your To-Do List, don't plan to do more than one thing at a time. Our gurus admit that most adults can complete a variety of unrelated tasks on any given day, but they say most of us can only do one thing at a time *well.*

Edward Hallowell says multitasking is like trying to play tennis with two balls, or three or four. He says it is a myth that you can perform two tasks simultaneously as well as you can perform them one at a time. You may feel an adrenaline rush, but you will not be performing all tasks equally well. Some task or tasks are getting less than your full attention and effort.

Every time you add a task, you dilute the attention you are providing to all tasks. Hallowell also notes that there really is no such thing as multitasking. You aren't really doing several things at the same time. You are just jumping from one task to another in rapid sequence. The exception to this is when you are working on a routine task you can perform on autopilot. Even then, you are probably not performing the task on autopilot as well as you could. Maybe you are performing it well enough, or think you are, but you are leaving something out whether you realize it or not. His recommendation: Never try to multitask when you are doing something important.

(Hallowell 2006, pp. 18-22)

Julie Morgenstern says people who multitask actually end up taking longer to complete each task than if they simply focused on one task at a time. She cites research that it takes your brain four times longer to recognize and process information when you are constantly switching from one task to another as you are when you multi-task. Consequently, when you multi-task, you aren't more productive, you are less productive.

(Morgenstern 2004, p. 102; Emmett 2009, pp. 107-109 makes the same point.)

While they don't recommend that you plan to multi-task, our gurus do recommend that you "Chuck" similar tasks together for clarity and focus—For example, answering email, handling physical mail, making phone calls. You may want to block out specific times of each day when you allocate time to perform these routine tasks. [See our discussion on handling email, phone calls, etc. later in this book.]

Schedule your highest priority/most-important task for the period of the day when you have the highest energy level. Donald Wetmore says consider whether you are a Morning Bird or Night Owl.

Morning birds have their highest energy level early in the day.

Night owls don't really get going until the afternoon or even at night.

Schedule the most important tasks for the time of the day when you are at your peak." Morning Birds should schedule important tasks in the morning, Night Owls should wait until later in the day.

(Wetmore 2005, pp. 33-34)

==

ARE YOU A MORNING BIRD OR NIGHT OWL?

TAKE THIS QUIZ

	YES	NO
Do you generally wake up at or before dawn?		
Is breakfast a big part of your day?		
Do you feel more alert and energetic in the morning before 10AM?		
Do you start feeling sleepy around 1PM or a little after?		
Do you find it hard to stay focused if must attend a meeting much after 3PM?		
Do you usually go to bed by 10PM or even earlier?		

HOW TO SCORE:

Score 1 point for each YES answer.

A score of four or higher indicates you are probably a Morning Bird, less than four you are probably an Owl.

(Based on a quiz suggested by Patricia Haddock in Haddock 2001, pp. 134-139)

==

Steve Prentice says the three best times for most people are:

- 9:00AM to 10:00AM

- 10:45-11:30AM (assuming they have had a mid-morning snack and break)

- 1:00PM-2:00PM (if they have had a lunch break)

Prentice says you should schedule important meetings for these Golden Hours.

What if you have to do something at a time of day that is wrong for you? Elaine St. James says if you have to undertake a task at a time of day when you are not at your maximum energy level, schedule to take a 10-minute nap before you engage in the activity. She suggests that you keep a roll-up pad, blanket and timer in your workspace. When you need to re-charge, put a "Do Not Disturb" sign on the door, roll out your map, set your timer for 10 minutes, lie down and close your eyes. When the timer goes off, get up and go back to work. St. James says a short 10-minute nap may be all it takes to get you back to maximum energy and efficiency.

(St. James 2001, pp. 118-119)

Donald E. Wetmore says that instead of starting your day with your most important tasks, you might begin with some easy tasks that take little time to complete. He says doing a few quick items first thing in the morning gives you a quick start on the day where you accomplish something right away.

(Wetmore 2005 pp. 27)

Our gurus caution that you should be sure to coordinate your To-Do list with others—family members, team members, etc.

Keep your To-Do list displayed where you can easily see it throughout the day—on top of your desk, displayed on your computer desktop, etc.. —Carry it with you wherever you go and consult it often. Check items off your list as you complete them each day.

At the end each day, make a list for the next day carrying over any uncompleted tasks and adding new ones. Purge any uncompleted tasks that have gotten on your To-Do list that you no longer need to do, make no difference to you or anyone else, or are things you have delegated to someone else. [See our discussion on How to Delegate later in this book.]

End each day by preparing your next day's To-Do list. Many successful people make writing their next day "To Do" list the last thing they do before they go to bed at night. They claim knowing what they have to do and having a plan for getting the important things in their life helps them sleep better. Susan St. James says spend just three minutes reviewing the day that has just ended. Think about anything that didn't go right that day. Maybe you didn't finish a task that you needed to complete. Maybe you had a disagreement with a co-worker. Now, says St. James, imagine that issue being resolved in a positive way. Ask your subconscious for help in finding a positive resolution. She says you may even want to write your request down in a journal you keep under your pillow. When you wake up in the morning, grab a piece of paper or your sleep journal and start writing something like "What I need to do to resolve that problem from yesterday is....." and let your subconscious take over from there. You may be amazed, says St. James, that while you were asleep your subconscious has worked out a solution.

(St. James 2001, pp. 124-125)

Brian Tracy makes a similar argument. He says one good reason to prepare your daily To-Do list the night before is that your brain will get started on the To-Do list right away. "When you plan your day the night before, your subconscious then goes to work on your plans and goals while you are asleep. Very often you will wake up in the morning with ideas and insights that apply to the work of the day."

(Tracy *Time* Power, 2007 p. 64)

Steve Prentice, author of *Cool Time*, recommends that you use what he calls an "I-Beam" approach to your daily agenda/To-Do List. Bracket the day with two short planning sessions, one at the beginning of the day and one at the end where you work out "realistically and pragmatically" your plan for the day. The bottom of the I-Beam comes at the end of the day where you spend 15 minutes doing some post-planning, summing up what you have accomplished and making note of those things that you need to focus on tomorrow. He suggests that part of this summing up time at the end of the day you should devote to analyzing what went right and wrong. Was that meeting necessary? How could you have better handled that interruption? Find mini-improvements in your time management plan.

(Prentice 2005 pp. 41-52)

Edward Hallowell says that the real purpose of spending time to plan your day is to find your rhythm. He writes: "When you find your rhythm, you don't plan everything you're doing; you're just doing it. You'll be in the zone. Just as a pianist who knows a piece so well that his cerebellum takes care of hitting the right notes can devote his conscious attention to other matters like expression and shading, so you can devote your conscious mind to higher issues than the nuts and bolts of each day if you have found the right rhythm for you."

(Hallowell 2006, p. 50)

TOOL #2: OVERCOME PROCRASTINATION

Do you ever find yourself having these thoughts when faced with a task on your To-Do list?

- "I've got to start soon."

- "I should have started earlier."

- "There is still time. I can still get it done."

- "Why bother? It's hopeless. I can't finish anyway."
- "Might as well just quit trying."
- "I will NOT do this to myself again."

If so, you may have experienced a bout of procrastination.

No matter how rigorous you are in making and attending to your To-Do list, chances are you will find yourself putting off tackling some activities. You will just keep moving them from one day's list to another. In short, you will procrastinate. You're not alone. We all procrastinate at least some of the time. In this section, we are going to discuss tips and techniques for overcoming procrastination.

---

pro·cras·ti·nate

Verb \prə-ˈkras-tə-ˌnāt, prō-\: *to put off intentionally the doing of something that should be done*

WHY DO PEOPLE PROCRASTINATE?

Here are the most common reasons why people procrastinate according to our gurus:

Fear:

Often people put off doing something simply out of fear. They are so afraid of how things will turn out that they just can't undertake the task. Fear comes in a variety of forms say our gurus including:

- **Fear of Failure:** No one wants to fail. It is personally disappointing and failing in public is embarrassing and humiliating. It is therefore not surprising that people would put off undertaking a task when they think they have little chance of succeeding.

- **Fear of Success:** Surprisingly, some people procrastinate because they are afraid of success, not failure. They think, "If I succeed in this task, people will just expect more. I'll have to perform even better next time." Or, "If I complete this task then I'll have to go on to the next task or project plan and the next and the next. I just don't have the stamina. It is just too much."

- **Fear of Being Judged:** "If I complete that task, someone is going to come along and want to evaluate how well I've done it. I might get a poor grade. If I don't try, there is nothing for them to judge."

- **Perfectionism:** Some people are just never satisfied with doing something right, they have to do it absolutely right. They must do everything flawlessly. Since no one can expect to do everything perfectly, the simple solution is to avoid undertaking anything where less-than-perfect performance is possible.

- **Feeling Overwhelmed:** The size, complexity or importance of the task just overwhelms people sometimes. The task just seems too challenging for them to even attempt.

- **Getting Stuck:** Sometimes everything starts out well and then problems arise. You do not know how to proceed and you cannot think of a person to ask for advice or a source to go to that might help you decide what to do next. You quit trying, not because you do not want to finish the task, but because you do not know how to finish it.

- **Feeling Bored:** This is the opposite of being overwhelmed. Sometimes people put off a task because it offers NO challenge. They may start the task, but quit halfway through simply because they find it so dull they can't force themselves to continue.

- **Hating the Task:** Sometimes, the task is just unpleasant. Maybe the working conditions are dirty, smelly or otherwise unpleasant. Maybe the task involves engaging with someone you do not like. Maybe completing the task could result in an unpleasant confrontation or hurt feelings.

(Sources of "Why People Procrastinate": Felton & Sims 2009, pp. 90-101; Haddock 2001, pp. 105-125; Leeds 2009, pp. 107-109; Silber 1998, pp. 98-99 & 101-106; and Tullier 2000, pp. 44-53 & 69-75.)

TIPS, TOOLS AND TECHNIQUES TO HELP YOU STOP PROCRASTINATING

Our gurus off a variety of advice for overcoming procrastination depending upon the reason you are procrastinating.

What to do if you procrastinate because you fear failure, success or being judged

Michelle Tullier says if you procrastinate because you fear failure, success or being judged you need some positive self-talk. Recall times in the past when you have faced a similar or related situation and dealt with it successfully. Success breeds success. Remembering when you faced your fears can help you boost your confidence. You did it before; you can do it again.

Imagine the worst-case scenario. What's the worst that could happen to you if you fail? Often it isn't as bad as it first seems. What's the chance that the worst will happen? In reality, the likelihood of the worst outcome may be very small. Ask yourself what you can do to prepare for the worst. What can you do to make the worst case LESS damaging or at least be prepared for it should it happen?

Imagine yourself succeeding. What would it feel like to hear the applause and congratulations from those who matter to you for a job well done? Use positive self-talk like the following.

Instead of....	Say....
I don't think I can do that.	I know it seems difficult, but I can get it done.
I can't get that done on time.	If I make this a priority, I can get it done on time.
I know I can't.	I think I can.

(Tullier 2000, pp. 155-156)

What to do if you procrastinate because you are seeking perfection

Our gurus say you should ask yourself if you are being realistic. Is it THAT important that you perform the task perfectly? Someone once asked the comedian Steve Allen how he had been able to accomplish so much. He said, "I have an almost total disregard for quality." We are not suggesting that you do sloppy work or ignore quality, but no one is perfect and you don't have to do most things perfectly. Often, OK IS good enough and indeed much better than NOT AT ALL. 98% and 100% right really aren't that different when it comes to most things. In baseball, no one considers a player who can hit three out of every ten pitches a failure. We consider him a HERO.

Julie Morgenstern says when she first started accepting speaking engagements and didn't hit the bull's eye with every performance she was crushed. She says she was surprised to find that the feedback she got was usually good even when she felt her performance had been sub-par. How could it be that she felt her performance was far less than what she wanted, but the audience still liked it and found it useful? Morgenstern says she discussed this perplexing phenomenon with a more seasoned speaker by the name of Jamie at a National Speakers Association convention one summer. Morgenstern says her friend Jamie gave her words of wisdom she has never forgotten. "Jamie knew what a perfect performance felt like, but had come to the realization that it was impossible to hit a 10 every time. Because he was a trained speaker with well-developed material, he'd learned to trust his skill set. His audience would enjoy and garner something from his speech, even if it was less than perfect. So each time he spoke, he figured as long as he hit at least a 7 (which was also excellent-the audience could never tell the difference between a 7 and a 10), he could live with himself and feel good about his performance."

(Morgenstern 2004, pp. 122-123)

Look at your SMART goals

Your greatest effort should go toward achieving your most important goals. Morgenstern says you might want to start being less perfect when it comes to tackling a lower-stake task, something you know really doesn't have to be done all that perfect. She says you may be surprised to find that, at least on many less-than-critical tasks, your version of "good, but not perfect" may be someone else's version of great.

(Morgenstern 2004, pp. 122-123)

Learn when to back away

Morgenstern says: "When you work on something for too long without any breaks, you reach the point of diminishing returns: the state in which you spend hours and hours getting almost nothing done, or worse, fixing things that weren't broken by second guessing your first, best impulses. Recognize when you are reaching that point and force yourself to back away. It will save you hours of futile effort and time spent redoing work done in a fog of poor judgment. Better yet, get a second opinion. Hearing what one or two people say, whose opinions you respect, is a way to give yourself some distance and perspective."

(Morgenstern 2004, pp. 122-123)

What to do if you procrastinate because you are overwhelmed or stuck

If you procrastinate because you are stuck and don't know how to go forward or the task seems so big and complex that you are overwhelmed, our gurus say you might want to try some of the following tricks to get unstuck.

Break the big task down into small tasks

Break large/complex projects down into smaller and smaller tasks. Focus on completing each small task. You will gain confidence as you finish each small task and eventually you will complete the larger project.

(Haddock 2001, p. 118)

Focus on DO dates, not DUE dates

Michelle Tullier, author of *The Complete Idiot's Guide to Overcoming Procrastination,* says the reason people end up putting things off to the last minute is that they focus too much on DUE dates and not enough on DO dates. DUE dates are the deadlines, the date, usually set by others, when you must turn something in, hand it over, mail or email it, or just stop working on it. DO dates are the specific days or times when you schedule on your calendar or To-Do list to complete a certain task. DO dates, says Tullier, are where the ACTION is and that's where you should focus. Take care of the DO dates and you will never have to worry about the DUE dates.

(Tullier 2000, pp. 156-157

"Salami Slice" the task

If you are unsure where to start, just start anywhere. Many large and complex projects involve steps/activities that you do not have to complete in any definite order. Brian Tracy says you should "Salami Slice" the task. He argues that —"Sometimes the best way to complete a major job is to take a small slice and complete just that piece, just as you would take a single slice of salami and eat it. Alternatively, use the "Swiss

Cheese" Technique—Punch holes in it. Select a five-minute part of the job and do only that." Many writers know that it is impossible to write a whole book at once but that they can manage the task if they just write one page a day. Before long, they finish the book, one page at a time.

(Tracy *Time Power* 2007, pp. 169-176)

How do you eat an elephant? One bite at a time.

Avoid "First this, then that"

Behavioral scientist Abraham Kaplan calls this the "ordinal fallacy." First, I will learn everything about skiing and then I will ski. First, I will learn everything about writing and then I will write a book. First, I will learn everything about doing this job just right, and then I will undertake the task. Since we can never learn everything about anything, we never get anything done. One thing must always happen if you are going to get anything done. You have to START... somewhere. As Kaplan says, "Whether it be due to a human failing or to the human condition, we must do as we aspire from the very beginning, or else resign ourselves to not doing at all."

(See Abraham Kaplan, *The Conduct of Social Inquiry*, San Francisco: Chandler Publishing, 1964, p. 402)

"The best time to plant a tree was 20 years ago. The second best time is now." – *Chinese Proverb (Griessman 1994, p. 78)*

One way to get started is to schedule a time to start working on whatever it is you are procrastinating about doing. Set aside 30 minutes or an hour to start. You don't have to spend a whole day; all you have to do is commit to spending those 30 minutes to an hour working on what you need to finish. You can then go on to something you find more enjoyable.

De-clutter

When you are stuck in the middle of completing a task, look around to see if the problem just might be clutter. If your orderly workplace is now a mess, you need to clean up. Put some order back into your workplace.

Take a break

Go for a walk. Take a shower. Do something else. Creative people say when they are stuck for an idea; they often get inspiration from taking a break. The interesting thing is that while they take a break, their mind does not. It just keeps thinking and suddenly they have a eureka moment. Arthur Fry, the 3M engineer who came up with the idea for Post-it Notes says his moment of inspiration came while he was daydreaming in church. His bookmark kept falling out of his hymnal when he dozed off. His mind connected that with a new glue a colleague of Fry's had developed that was a failure. It was so weak it would barely hold two pieces of paper together. It suddenly occurred to Fry that that his colleague's lousy glue would make a perfect bookmark, one that would stay put but come off easily.

Elaine St. James recommends a 10-minute walk as the best cure for being stuck. She says you should walk briskly and take deep breaths. Focus on what you see and feel. Is it hot or cold, windy or still? Observe the sky, the trees, the traffic, and the people around you. Forget the problem that has you stuck. Try not to think about anything but your immediate surroundings for these 10 minutes. Go back to work when the 10 minutes are up. You may be surprised to find that while you were focusing on the sky and trees, your mind was hard at work solving the problem. Suddenly, the solution is obvious. You know how to proceed. Even if that doesn't happen, what have you lost? You have taken a much-needed break.

(St. James 2001, pp. 100-103)

Seek help

It seems so obvious but sometimes the solution to being stuck or overwhelmed is that we just need to ask for help. Talk to someone, even if that person is not an expert on the topic. Sometimes all you need is someone who will listen and help you sort through what's got you stuck. All you may need is some handholding—someone to keep you company, cheer you up, help you sort through the clutter, and so on.

What to do if you procrastinate because you are bored or the task in unpleasant

Set a schedule

Earlier we noted that Julie Morgenstern said you should schedule the task you would be most thrilled to complete early in the morning. Other gurus say that it is usually best to schedule the distasteful things EARLY in the day since once you tackle the most distasteful thing you have to do then the rest of your day just gets better and better.

Eat your frogs for breakfast

Brian Tracy says if you start your day with the biggest or most difficult or most unpleasant task first and stick with it until you complete it, then the remaining tasks you have to perform throughout the rest of the day will just get easier. Tracy quotes Mark Twain: "If the first thing you do each morning is eat a live frog, you can go through the day with the satisfaction of knowing that that is probably the worst thing that is going to happen to you all day long." Tracy says that the first rule in frog eating is: If you have to eat two frogs, eat the ugliest one first. The second rule says Tracy is to take action immediately. After all, if you have to eat a live frog, it does not help to sit and look at it too long. Don't think about it. Just grab that ugly frog and start chewing.

(Tracy *Eat That Frog* 2007, pp. 2-3)

Find freedom in routine

Michelle Tullier recommends that you pick a time of the day or the week to take care of all the routine and boring stuff. You are then free the rest of the day or week to do things that are more interesting.

(Tullier 2000, p. 153)

Do a little bit at a time

Tackle a little bit of the distasteful task at a time. Tell yourself you don't have to spend forever on this thing you don't want to do, just 15 minutes or 30 minutes or an hour. Note: Tracy and Twain might disagree about this. See "eat your frogs for breakfast" earlier.

Make it more pleasant

Is there a way to make the unpleasant task more pleasant? For example, you have to complete a report you really don't want to write. Can you work on it in more pleasant surroundings? For example, maybe you can take your laptop to the park and work on the report there. Put some honey or ketchup on your frogs.

Be creative

Instead of just doing nothing toward completing the unpleasant task find, something else you can do related to your overall goal that you like better. For example, you are procrastinating about writing a report. Instead of avoiding the unpleasant report writing task by chatting with coworkers, find something related to the task to do that you find less pleasant. For example, you assemble some of the data you will need to complete the report.

Reward yourself

Think of something you would really like to do or something you really want. Make completing the unpleasant task a condition for getting that reward.

Swap tasks

When you need to complete an unpleasant task, maybe you can swap with someone who doesn't find that task unpleasant. You hate house cleaning, but love to garden. Your neighbor hates gardening (but enjoys the fresh vegetables) but doesn't mind cleaning. Therefore, you swap. The neighbor does the cleaning for both of you and you do the gardening.

(Haddock 2001, p. 122)

A Contrarian View: It is OK to Procrastinate Sometimes

Brian Tracy says that sometimes you should procrastinate on purpose. In fact, he says you have to procrastinate on something since you cannot do everything. You will have to put some things off until later or not do them at all. Just make sure you procrastinate on the unimportant things. You want to do conscious procrastination, not unconscious procrastination. Tracy said think of it as practicing "Creative Procrastination." "Because you cannot do everything, you have to procrastinate on many things, if not most things. Creative procrastination requires that you deliberately decide, on a conscious level, the items you are going to put off doing so that you have more time to do those things that really make a difference in your life." Tracy says when you practice creative procrastination you will quickly find out that 80% of the items on your To-Do list are really of low value and can safely be put off, leaving more time for you to concentrate on the 20% of items that are really valuable.

(Tracy *Eat That Frog* 2007, pp. 33-35 & p. 83)

TOOL # 3: HANDLE INTERRUPTIONS

Interruptions are unanticipated events. Something happens that you weren't expecting. You get a phone call; receive an email, someone drops by that you didn't expect to see. Suddenly, you can no longer continue doing what you planned.

Donald Wetmore notes that there are good and bad interruptions. Good interruptions are by definition critical and important. Something has come up that requires your attention. Bad interruptions disrupt your schedule for something that has little or no value.

(Wetmore 2005, pp. 79-84)

Good interruptions are not the problem. Bad interruptions are. So how do you get rid of, or at least reduce, the number of bad interruptions? Our gurus say you should tackle interruptions in two steps:

Step One: Keep an interruptions log

Wetmore says you should keep an Interruptions Log for a week and record any interruptions you experience, good or bad. Record each interruption with the date and time, who are what interrupted you, the length of the interruption and a notation whether it was a good or bad interruption.

Interruptions Log

Date/Time	Who/What	Length	Good/Bad
6/11: 10AM	John—Game last night	30	B
6/11: 2PM	Gary-Customer Question	15	G

Review your interruptions log at the end of the week and look for patterns

- Did most of the interruptions occur at a certain time of day or week?
- Who interrupted you and how often?
- What—Does some issue come up repeatedly
- Length—Did you have several long interruptions or many short ones?
- Rating—What was the ratio of Good to Bad interruptions?

(Wetmore 2005, pp. 79-84)

STEP TWO: REDUCE BAD INTERRUPTIONS

Use one of more of the following techniques to reduce the number of BAD interruptions, particularly recurring ones.

NOTE: All of these recommendations work equally well at home as at work, particularly if you ever work at home.

Prevent BAD interruptions from occurring

The best way to deal with bad interruptions is to stop them before they ever start. Here are some tips.

- Tell people you are working on something important and do not want to be interrupted except in an emergency. Do not interrupt other people when they are busy.

- Put a "Do NOT Interrupt unless it is REALLY IMPORTANT" sign of the door to your workspace. Jan Yager says the sign should read "The genius is BUSY" and the flips side of that sign should read, "The genius is FREE now."

- Close the door to your workspace or go to a different area of the building—an empty office or classroom, for example—where people won't expect to find you.

- Turn your desk or workspace so that you are facing AWAY from the door. People will be less likely to interrupt you if they have trouble getting your attention. **Tip:** Consider discretely placing a mirror so you can see with a glance who might be at the door. If you want to see them, you can respond. If not, use your body language to make it clear you are focused on something important. Steve Prentice says you should keep your body facing your work. If you seated at your desk, don't stand up. Don't make eye contact; just raise your eyes or eyebrows. Keep your body language "closed" on your work. Even better, you could use a prop such as a telephone headset to suggest that you are possibly on the phone and can't be disturbed.

(Prentice 2005, pp. 122-126)

- Pay attention to other sources of distraction having to do with the arrangement of your workspace, for example

- o If you are a visual learner, having your desk at a window may not be a good idea.

- o If you are an auditory learner, working in a noisy place may affect your concentration.

- o If touch/feel is your thing, working in a place that is too warm or cold may affect your concentration.

- Don't put out a bowl of candy or anything else that would entice people to just drop-in.

- Remove the visitor's chairs from your work area or stack papers/books on them so people won't be encouraged to sit down and stay awhile.

- Keep supplies other people need access to away from your work area so they can get what they need without interrupting you.

- Schedule a time to receive phone calls, answer email, respond to voice mail and text messages and stick to it. You don't have to take every call or answer every message immediately. If possible, identify someone people can contact who can interrupt you IF and ONLY IF the call or message is critically important. Elaine St. James says you should be very discriminating in giving out your cell phone number AND, NO, you are under no obligation to take every call--"Just because other people choose to be available around the clock, it doesn't mean you have to."

- Use your cell phone to get help if you need it or to communicate with coworkers and family members when there's a change of plans. However, be sure to ask others not to overuse it. In addition, turn it off when you don't want people to interrupt you.

Establish work hours when you will receive phone calls and stick to them.

- Don't give out your cell phone or your home number if you can avoid doing so. When you must give out your number, set limits on when you'll be available: "If you must call me at home, I'm available between 8 and 10 P.M. Monday through Thursday." "Please don't call me after 10 P.M." "Please don't call me on weekends unless it's urgent." You have to control when, who and if people will be able to interrupt you with a cell phone call, or any phone call for that matter.

- Turn off your cell phone and the pop-up box or ringtone for email and messages when you need to concentrate. St. James says if you have a few people who you want to be able to contact you anytime they need you, like your kids or an ailing parent, then get a second inexpensive cell phone just for that purpose and never, ever give out that special number to anyone.

(St. James 2001, pp. 47-49)

- Patricia Haddock says when you leave a telephone message on someone's voice mail tell the person you are trying to reach when you will be available to take a return call so that you can avoid playing "telephone tag." In addition, she says you should leave your full telephone number, including area code, so the person does not have to look up that information.

(Haddock 2001, p. 78)

- Encourage people to use email rather than phoning so that you can respond at your convenience rather than theirs.

- Turn off your phone and let people leave messages by voice mail. Steve Prentice says your voice mail message should:

  o Include the date the message was recorded,

  o Be changed daily,

  o Say it is okay for the caller to leave a detailed message so that you will have the information you need to respond,

  o Let the caller know when they can expect to get a call back—tell them when you will be reviewing your voice mail and returning calls, and

  o Be upbeat and positive—sound as if you are happy to hear from them (even if you aren't).

  Prentice provides this example: "You've reached Steve Prentice of ABC Company at extension 123 for Tuesday the 16th. I will be in a meeting this morning and will be returning calls after 11:00 AM. Please feel free to leave a detailed voice message of up to two minutes, and I will get back to you as promised. If this message is urgent, please press zero to reach my assistant. Thank you."

(Prentice 2005, p. 123)

Dealing with interruptions when they occur

Of course, no matter what you do or say some people are just going to interrupt you anyway. Strange as it may seem, some people like interruptions. They get a break from what they are doing. They may feel important or needed because someone wanted to talk to them or get their help. Often these are the very people who will interrupt you. They will probably show up repeatedly on your Interruptions Log. You are probably never going to get them to stop interrupting you completely, but here are some ideas our Gurus offer for minimizing the damage interrupters can do to your time management.

When someone drops by unexpectedly, stand up and meet them at the door. Invite them in only if the issue is important enough for you to take time to discuss it then. Don't let them get comfortable. Keep them standing.

(Haddock 2001, pp. 98-99)

If it looks like they want to stay and chat and you don't have the time, ask them to walk with you to the copy machine, soda or coffee machine or while you complete some other minor errand. Let them talk while you complete the errand, then make an excuse and leave them while you return to your work area.

Set a time limit and stick to it. Tell the drop-in that you are busy and have a lot to do, but that you can give them a few minutes if it is important, otherwise schedule a later time when you can meet with them to discuss the matter. Say: "I have only about four or five minutes at the moment. We can start discussing this now and, if we don't get finished in that amount of time, we continue at a later time if you like." Stick to the time limit you have set.

(Griessman 1994, pp. 116-118)

When time is up, provide a verbal or non-verbal clue that your visitor should wrap it up. Start looking for something in a file drawer or on your desk to send a message that you are distracted and no longer really listening to what the interrupter is saying. Get papers together, pick up your purse, put on your coat or take other actions that signal that you need to leave. Get rid of the unexpected guest and go for a short walk. Eugene Griessman says you could say something like this to speed the conversation along, "I know you are a busy person, so let me ask you one final quick question."

(Griessman 1994, pp 116-118)

Haddock calls these "wrap up" phrases. "Let's wrap this up." "We'll have to continue this later."

(Haddock 2001, pp. 98-99)

If the drop-in wants to tell you a long story say, "That's very interesting and I would like to hear all about it. Let's have lunch tomorrow when I can give you my full attention. Where would you like to go for lunch?" **Note:** You can always cancel the lunch later if you really aren't interested in the story.

If you know a particular individual is a chronic interrupter, arrange to have someone call you or interrupt your conversation with the drop in to remind you that you are going to be late to an important meeting. Use a "fake phone call" AP to receive a fake phone call after a few minutes to "remind" you of something urgent that needs your attention.

If the matter is routine, ask the person to reserve it until the meeting where you typically deal with non-critical issues so that everyone who should have input on the issue can be involved.

Have a prepared close and use it. Say: "Well, it has been great talking to you, but I really have to go. I'll get back to you soon. (Pause) Thanks." Then go. Alternatively, "I've really enjoyed chatting, but I really need to talk to the man/woman over there before they leave." (Smile and move on.)

If what looked like a short question is turning into a much bigger issue, say, "You know when you started telling me about this it seemed pretty simple but, now it seems to be a little more complicated than I first thought. I think we need to schedule some time later when we can both focus on this issue. What time would be best for you tomorrow or later this week?" Get out your calendar and schedule the meeting.

Refer them to another person. If you don't think you are the best person to handle the issue the intruder wants to discuss or if you just don't have the time to discuss it at the moment, say: "Jane, I would like to help you out on that but I just don't think I'm the right person to give you advice at this moment. Why don't you see Mary, she is good with this type of thing? I can call her to see if she is free if you like."

TOOL #4: LEARN TO DELEGATE

When you take on too much, you waste time on tasks that others should or could perform. In this section, we discuss time management techniques that will help you free up time to focus on your SMART goals by delegating the task to someone else.

WHY PEOPLE HAVE PROBLEMS DELEGATING

Have you ever found yourself working on tasks that you knew someone else should be performing and might even be able to perform better than you might, but you still couldn't let go? You just somehow felt you had to do the job yourself. You couldn't delegate even when you knew you should. Alec Mackenzie, author of *The Time Trap* says that seven primary reasons people have problems delegating:

Ego

Face it; you just think you can do the job better. Mackenzie says that may be true, but when you don't delegate you not only waste your time, but you don't give the other person the opportunity to learn.

Anxiety about mistakes

You fear that if you let someone else do the job, he or she won't perform the job right. You'll just have to pick up the pieces and fix what they messed up. That may be true, says Mackenzie, but when there is no opportunity for mistakes, there is no opportunity for growth. The truth is people learn through failure. You've heard the saying, "Nothing risked, nothing gained." It is true, particularly when it comes to delegating and time management.

Comfort level

Not delegating could just be a form of procrastination. Mackenzie says new managers in particular, often fail to delegate because they are more comfortable performing the task a subordinate could perform than performing their new and more complex duties.

Fear of loss of control

Some people have a problem with delegating because they have difficulty letting go. They fear they will lose control if they turn something over to someone else.

Desire for perfection

Your parents probably taught you this rule: "If anything is worth doing, it's worth doing well." Since your ego tells you that you can do the job better than anyone can, you have to do it if it is really going to be done right. Mackenzie says you should lighten up. Remember when we discussed procrastination, we noted that perfection isn't always necessary. It might not even be desirable when you consider the cost. Learn to accept "good enough" since, in fact, in many cases "good enough" is good enough. Save perfect for when it is truly important.

False sense of efficiency

Have you ever thought something like this when deciding whether to delegate a task: "I can do this is a half an hour or less; if I let Mary do it, I'll just have to show her how and then she will take all day. Better just get busy and do it myself and get it done." Sure, says Mackenzie, you may be able to do the job faster and better this time, but if you never let Mary try, she will never learn to do it. You will have to do it every time and you will never free yourself to focus on what you should be doing.

(Mackenzie 1997, pp. 115-117)

EFFECTIVE DELEGATION

Mackenzie says the reason most people have a problem with delegating is that they get one or more of the six steps to effective delegation wrong. He says if you neglect any one of these steps, you are inviting miscommunication, misunderstandings, demoralization and poor performance. Mackenzie's five steps are:

Step One: Match the person to the job.

The best predictor of whether a person can do a job well is past performance. If they have successfully done it in the past, they should be able to do it as well, or even better, this time. However, that doesn't mean that you shouldn't let a novice try. You will just have to pay more attention to the remaining four steps.

Step Two: Give clear instructions.

This step is particularly important if the person being delegated the task is a novice. Novice or not, you need to define the standards of success. You should go over the critical steps and decision points in getting the job done right and have the person repeat back what they heard to make sure that they understand.

Step Three: Given them commensurate authority.

The worst thing you can do is to assign someone responsibility for performing a task and then withhold from them the authority to obtain whatever they need to do the job—financial resources, assistance from others, equipment, information, or anything else. Set them up for success, not failure.

Step Four: Follow-up.

Establish checkpoints. Break the job down into steps and make sure you get progress reports at each stage. If the person delegated the task is getting off track or running behind schedule, you can take action to correct the problem before it gets out of hand. If things are going well, you and the person delegated the task will have less stress.

Step Five: Coach but don't over control.

Find the right balance between providing the assistance and advice the person needs to succeed in the task and over controlling. People can't do their best work if they feel you are looking over their shoulder at every moment. On the other hand, you need to step in when they are stuck or it is obvious that they are getting off track. Your goal is to help them succeed so that they will eventually learn to perform the task with little or no assistance from you at all.

(Mackenzie 1997, pp. 117-119)

(NOTE: See also, Tracy 2007, pp. 212-213;
Yager 1999, pp. 103-107 and Griessman 1994, pp. 139-143
for more on delegation.)

TOOL #5: LEARN TO SAY NO

Lee Silber, author of *Time Management for the Creative Person*, says the greatest time saver of all is one word—NO.

Silber admits that saying "NO" often causes problems, if nothing more than hurt feelings. However, failing to say "NO" often enough has even worse consequences.

- *You end up becoming a jack-of-all-trades, master of none. Everything you do ends up being a rush job, and nothing is done particularly well or on time.*
- *While you are busy helping others with their projects, your own more important projects and commitments suffer.*
- *Eventually you end up being overcommitted and burned out. You have no time left to be creative as you rush from project to project.*
- *You end up being seen as a flake because you can't finish things on time...*
- *You end up regretting your decisions and resent the person you agreed to help out.*
- *You take on projects and assignments that may be unethical, immoral, or illegal because you were afraid to say "no."*

(Silber 1998, pp. 237-238)

Eugene Griessman says when you don't say NO, you take someone else's "Monkey." A "Monkey" is a problem or task. Some people want to unload their monkeys on you. Monkeys can be bad mannered, nasty, tiresome and real time consumers. Additionally, Monkeys like to jump from the backs of their rightful owners to other people's backs. Soon you will end up with a back full of monkeys mostly other people's. Griessman says when someone tries to give you their monkey, you should listen, but don't volunteer to take their monkey unless it is a monkey you really, really care about. Insist that people come to you not just with complaints and problems but with possible solutions, you can help them sort through. Just say NO—Avoid meetings, appointments and social events that are a waste of time. Say, "I'm sorry, but I won't be able to help you this time." Say, "Thank you for the invitation to get involved, but I have only so much time available and have to make difficult choices. I just can't take on anything more at this time." As a last resort, when you someone is a prime "monkey sharer," you can make yourself scarce. If they can't find you, they can't interrupt you or ask you to take on their monkey.

(Griessman 1994 pp. 109-114)

(For more on this see: Kenneth Blanchard, et. Al. *The One Minute Manager Meets the Monkey*, New York: Harper-Collins, 1989).

WHY IS IT SO HARD TO SAY "NO"?

Why is it so hard for most of us to say "NO"? Here are some reasons and reality checks offered by Michelle Tullier, author of *The Complete Idiot's Guide to Overcoming Procrastination*

You like to feel needed and feel a sense of obligation to help when you can. Anyway, you are flattered that someone asked for your help

Reality Check: It is fine to want to be of service to others, but it is wise to choose the obligations you undertake. You have no obligation to say YES always. Think of others, but also think about your own welfare.

You don't like confrontations and you want people to like you.

Reality Check: Ok, saying NO isn't the most enjoyable thing you will ever do and those you turn down may be disappointed. However, it is not the worst thing you will ever experience. Most people, even when disappointed, can and will accept NO for an answer. Anyway, you wouldn't be doing them a favor by taking on a task that you might not perform or be able to perform well.

You are afraid that if you say NO, you might miss out on a real opportunity

Reality Check: If this request truly offers you an opportunity to move closer to achieving your goals, go for it. However, think through the commitment you are making. Is the task as simple as it seems? Be realistic. If it is going to take time away from more important things, reconsider.

(Tullier 2000, pp. 111-112)

WHEN TO SAY NO

Alec Mackenzie and Pat Nickerson, authors of *The Time Trap*, 4th Edition, says you should definitely say NO (or at least not YES) in the following circumstances:

- Someone asks you to help him or her get out of a situation that arose from his or her own neglect, particularly after they have had repeated warnings. You don't help someone improve by constantly getting them out of jams.

- Someone asks you to do him or her a favor, but to do so you will have to neglect an item of higher priority. Postpone doing the favor until another day.

- Someone, even your boss, asks you to do something that you know is technically infeasible, impractical, or not cost effective. To offer better options.

- Someone is just trying to dump an unpleasant or tedious task on you because they don't want to do it themselves.

- Someone asks you to do something that's illegal or you find morally or ethically offensive.

- If the request doesn't contribute to your personal and professional SMART goals, then you should probably say NO.

(Mackenzie and Nickerson 2009, p. 99)

HOW TO SAY NO

So just how do you say "NO" without making an enemy of the person who wants you to say "YES?" Our gurus offer the following tips.

Turn down the request as soon as possible.

When you decide the request doesn't fit your SMART goals, say NO as soon as you can. Don't wait. The longer you wait the greater the chance that you will say YES when you should say NO and the harder it will be for the person you turn down to find someone else to help who can say YES.

Don't rush your decision.

While it is important to make a decision as soon as possible, don't' rush the decision if you are uncertain about saying YES at first. If you let people rush you to make a decision, you'll probably end up saying YES when you would have said NO if you had given it some more thought. When you have doubts about a request, sleep on it before you answer. Talk to someone you trust who can help you sort out the consequences of a YES.

Be polite but succinct when you say NO.

Don't go into detail about why you can't honor a request otherwise you will just be opening the door for the other person to try to find a way to fit the request into your schedule. Tullier suggests that you just say something like, "I thought about your request. I am flattered that you think I'm the right person to do this, but after giving it a lot of thought, I'm going to have to say NO." End it at that.

(Tullier 2000, p. 113)

Emmett suggests you say something like this:

"I'd love to do that, but not at this time..."

"Thank you for asking me. I'm honored and glad you asked; unfortunately I can't...."

"I'd love to do that. What day did you say it was? Sorry, I can't make it. I have plans." Merritt says don't go into detail about your plans since the person asking probably will not think your plans are more important.

(See Merrett 2009, pp. 157-159 for more "how to say NO" phrases.)

Never use "victim vocabulary."

Never say things like "I'm sorry...," "I wish I could but...," or "I'm very busy..." when turning down a request. Pat Nickerson says experienced manipulators will pounce on your non-assertive NO and you will soon find yourself agreeing to do the very thing you wanted to avoid.

(Mackenzie and Nickerson 2009, p. 100)

HOW TO GET OUT OF A COMMITMENT YOU HAVE ALREADY MADE

What do you do if you have already said YES and realize that you should have said NO?

There might not be much you can do if the project is important and people are counting on you. You may have to go ahead and just do the best you can do. Ideally, find a way to delegate some of the work to others. However, let's say the project isn't too far along and others could take over. Here are some tips Tullier has for getting out when you never should have gotten in:

- Don't wait. Get out as soon as you realize that you have made a mistake by saying YES.

- Explain that it is better that you leave now when someone can more easily step in and take your place rather than later when the project is farther along.

- Find or suggest a replacement.

- Offer to help your replacement get up to speed as fast as possible.

- Explain why you are bailing out. Show that you have valid reasons and aren't just abandoning your responsibility. You do have valid reasons, right?

- Explain that having someone involved who couldn't give their all to make the project a success would hurt the project.

(Tullier 2000, pp. 113-114)

Remember, everything you say "yes" to is a "no" to something else. Think about that for a minute. A "yes" at work can be a "no" to your family. A "yes" to a friend can mean a "no" to a lucrative offer at work. (Silber 1998, p. 238)

TOOL# 6: MANAGE MEETINGS

(Primary sources: Yager 1999, p. 111; Wetmore 2005, pp. 210-219; Hoover 2007, p. 83; Mackenzie 1997, pp. 149-154 and Griessman 1994, pp. 100-103.)

Meetings should be time savers. They can help you coordinate work with others, set goals, make decisions about how to expedite work, and solve problems getting in the way of getting the job done. Too often, however, meetings become time wasters. Here are some tips our gurus offer for making the meetings you hold and/or attend time savers and not time wasters.

NOTE: If you conduct a meeting, it is your responsibility to follow these effective meeting rules. If you attend a meeting, you should be proactive in insisting that the leader follows these rules.

RULES FOR EFFECTIVE MEETINGS

Don't meet if you can avoid it

If you do not absolutely need to hold a meeting, don't call one. You may be able to accomplish everything you need to accomplish though a conference call, video chat, email, etc.

Ask to be excused

If you don't think you are needed at a meeting, contact the person who invited you and explain that while you would like to attend you have pressing matters that you need to attend to such as finishing an important project and ask to be excused. Offer to send a written statement instead of attending in person.

Prepare and distribute a detailed agenda

If you call a meeting, provide those invited to attend with a detailed agenda in advance so they know the reason for the meeting and can come prepared to contribute. The detailed agenda should break the meeting down into timed segments so that all topics can be covered. It should specify exactly when the meeting will begin AND end. Ask attendees to bring all relevant information they think they might need given the meeting topics and that they give some thought to the topics of the meeting in advance so they are prepared to discuss them. If you are invited to a meeting and do not receive an agenda, contact the person who called the meeting to request one. Be polite. Just explain that you want to be sure to bring along any information that might be useful.

Use the Rickover agenda format

Alex McKenzie suggests that you consider using an agenda similar to the one used by Admiral Hyman Rickover, the four-star admiral who oversaw the development of America's nuclear submarine program. Rickover was famous for running effective meetings. He used an agenda that listed topics by starting time, with space to record decisions, assignments/responsibilities and deadlines for follow-up action during the course of the meeting. At the end of the meeting, Rickover simply crossed out the word "Agenda" and wrote, "Minutes" and had copies distributed to the appropriate people.

Place experts on call

Whether you run or attend a meeting, notify any people you might need to call upon for expert advice or assistance that they should hold themselves available during the time of the meeting to offer assistance in person or electronically if they are needed.

Dismiss early any attendee no longer needed

If you run a meeting, dismiss anyone once you discuss the topics of interest to them or for which you needed their attendance. If you attend a meeting, ask the meeting leader to excuse you when it is clear you are no longer needed at the meeting.

Have a strict start and stop time

If you call a meeting, be specific about exactly when the meeting will start and start on time even if not everyone has arrived. If you attend a meeting and it doesn't start on time, ask the person conducting the meeting if they could begin since you need to leave to attend to another matter as soon as the meeting is scheduled to end.

Cancel the meeting if key decision-makers can't attend

Cancel a meeting or suggest that it be canceled if critical decision-makers will not be able to attend.

Make the meeting room UNCOMFORTABLE.

For example, install uncomfortable chairs, eliminate refreshments, turn off the heat or cooling, have everyone stand. You don't want the attendees to want to stay any longer than it takes to hold the meeting.

Stick to the agenda and time schedule.

If you run a meeting, stick to the agenda and time schedule for the various segments. When new issues arise, make a note to take them up at a different time. If the time for a topic runs out, but it requires more discussion, end the discussion and schedule another meeting to deal specifically with that topic. If you attend a meeting and you find the discussion wandering off track, ask the leader if he could return to the agenda and/or suggest that the group take up some issues at another time. Decide who should attend this separate meeting to continue discussion on a particular topic. Often only a small number of the attendees at the first meeting will need to be involved in the continuing discussion by this focused sub-committee.

Get the timing and pacing right.

If you run or attend a meeting, pay attention to timing and pacing. Meetings should not be overly tense, competitive or time driven, nor should they be too soft, fuzzy or entertaining. A certain amount of tension between participants can help open up the discussion to new ideas. On the other hand, a too-tense moment sometimes benefits from a joke that provides some release.

Have someone take and transcribe the minutes.

If you run a meeting, designate someone in attendance to take the minutes and/or record the session and produce a written transcript. Request that the leader have this done if you are attending a meeting.

Conclude with a summary of key decisions

If you run a meeting, at the end summarize for the attendees what you think the meeting achieved and any agreements reached and/or assignments made. If a follow-up meeting and/or sub-committee meeting(s) will be required, specify when and where these meetings will occur and who should attend.

End on time.

Never run over the time limit for the meeting. If you need more time to discuss issues, call another meeting.

Distribute the minutes

Send a follow-up copy or at least a summary of the minutes of the meeting and summary of decisions and assignments made to all attendees the next day. Note:

If you used the Rickover agenda, you may be able to distribute just the ~~agenda~~ minutes. See our earlier discussion.

TOOL # 7: MANAGE YOUR PHYSICAL MAIL

It is a reality of life that one of your daily burdens will be handling physical mail. Some of it will bring you useful information or offers. Much of it will just be junk that clutters your home or workspace and wastes your time. Here are some tips from our Gurus for saving time by handling physical mail efficiently.

OPT OUT

Reduce the amount of mail you receive. Ask people who correspond with you to use email or text messages rather than physical mail. Get off junk mail lists by:

- Always unchecking the mailing list box when you sign up for a service, subscription, etc. This applies to email also.

- Never enter yourself into contests. If you do, request that contest holders NOT add your name to any mail or email list.

- Call 1-888-5 OPT OUT (1-888-567-8688) and request that name be removed from credit agencies' lists.

- Go to CatlogChoice.org or DMAchoice.org and request that your name be removed from direct marketing mailing lists.

SCHEDULE A TIME AND PLACE FOR HANDLING MAIL:

Set aside a specific time and place each day to handle physical mail. Most people make the mistake of flipping through the day's mail while they are doing something else. For example, as soon as they walk in their house or office they start opening mail while they are taking off their coat, pouring a cup of coffee and so on. They are NOT prepared to deal with their mail in an efficient manner because they lack the necessary tools:

- A shredder-To dispose of anything not needed or wanted that contains any personal information

- A recycling bin—To dispose of everything not needed or wanted that can be recycled.

- A filing system and calendar—To place mail requiring either immediate or future action.

TAKE ACTION

You should take immediate action on every piece of mail that was not shredded or recycled. The key to handling physical mail, like the key to efficiently handling all paper documents, is to handle each piece of paper only once. In most cases, this will involve:

- Responding immediately—Address items that require a simple response immediately. Write a short note; send a brief email, etc.

- Filing items for later response—Place items that require more thought in a pending file so you can address them later. Be sure to schedule time on your calendar.

- Filing items for long-term storage—You should file items that you need to retain for future reference such as legal documents in appropriate paper folders or scan them into electronic files.

TOOL # 8: MANAGE YOUR EMAIL

(Primary sources: Haddock 2001, p. 80; Hoover 2007, pp. 119-201; Leeds 2009, p. 185 and Wetmore 2007, pp. 119-121)

Email can be a great time saver or great time waster depending upon how you manage it. Here are some consensus tips our gurus offer for managing email others send to you and email you send to others.

MANAGING INCOMING EMAIL

Unsubscribe or remove your email address from unwanted or unread mailings.

Consider setting up different email boxes for different purposes—email from friends, business email, general email, etc.

Cut off email notifications and pop-up boxes or you will be checking email all day long and get nothing done.

Set aside a specific time each day to check your email. If you receive a lot of email and/or conduct important business by email, schedule to check it several times per day—first thing, mid-morning, mid-afternoon, at the end of the day, etc.

Schedule to check email at the time of the day when your energy and creativity level are at the lowest so that you can focus on tasks that are more important when you are at your best. See our earlier discussion of Early Birds and Night Owls.

Tell your boss, friends, etc. that you check email only at certain times of the day. If they have an urgent message and it is truly urgent, they should text instead.

Delete unnecessary messages before opening and reading other email.

Don't open or download email from strangers, particularly if they have attachments.

Use rules or filters in your email software to sort incoming email automatically into appropriate folders, or to delete unnecessary email entirely. Set up your email program to move suspected spam automatically to a separate folder.

Use the "Two-Minute" Rule in reading email. If you are confident you can write a response to an email in two minutes or less, respond right away. That's quicker than sorting it into a folder for later response.

Use templates or autoresponders to send standard replies to common email.

Sort the remaining email into folders according to broad action categories you need to take. For example, "Waiting Reply," "Reference," etc. Additionally, if you archive incoming email according to subject matter, it will be easier for you to find an email message later since you will only need to search in the relevant subject matter folder. **Tip:** Your email software may allow you to star or otherwise highlight messages awaiting a response.

Quickly look through the emails in your "waiting reply" folder and respond to the easy-to-answer emails first before focusing on email responses that will take more time or thought.

As a rule of thumb, if your email address is in the "CC" field of the incoming email rather than in the "TO" field, you may safely file it for later response. The sender is likely sending the message to you for information only and may not even require a response.

Download attachments to appropriate folders on your hard drive and delete the emails, including the attachments to avoid taking up unnecessary space on your email server.

Your goal in checking email should be to delete it, file it for later action, or reply/act on it immediately. Leave nothing in your inbox when you are finished.

MANAGING OUTGOING EMAIL

Set a good example. The more you use and follow good email formatting and use, the more likely others will do so also.

Keep it short. Say what you mean right away. Use as few words as you can. Be concise, clear and straightforward. Use short sentences and avoid complicated punctuation. It is not necessary to write in complete sentences or to use formal language if sentence fragments and simple words will do the job.

Proofread, proofread, and proofread. Ideally write a draft of your message in word processing software like Word. Proofread your message carefully and do a spell check. Only when you are confident that you have your message right should you copy and paste it into an email. Never send an email without proofreading the message first to make sure it says what you want to say and is professional.

Never send an email when you are angry. If you are angry or the subject matter is controversial, don't send a response right away. Sleep on it. Reread your response the next day before you send it. Is this the message you want to send? Is it clear? Could it be misinterpreted?

Treat every email like a billboard. Don't assume no one will read your email or that only the person you send it to will read it. Assume sending an email is like putting a message on a billboard everyone will see.

Never use all caps or exclamation marks. That's yelling. It's rude.

Don't be terse or abrupt or give commands. That's rude also.

Make the subject clear. Write clear and descriptive subject lines that ideally indicate a call to action. If you are forwarding a message, place your comments at the top above the email you received. If you place your comments below the email, the reader may miss them.

Be careful with bulk emails. Use "BCC" for bulk emails. When responding to bulk email, make sure you are replying only to those persons you intend to receive your reply and not to everyone who received the original email.

KEY IDEAS

- Manage your day with a prioritized and up-to-date To-Do List. Never leave home without it.

- Plan your day to handle the highest priority/most important tasks when you are at your highest energy level.

- Think hard about why you might be procrastinating. Is it because you are afraid of success or failure? Are you overwhelmed or stuck? Are you bored or hate the task? Follow our gurus' tips to get unstuck.

- Keep an interruptions log. Avoid interruptions if you can. Follow our gurus' tips for dealing with interruptions when they occur.

- Learn to delegate.

- Say "NO"

- Manage meetings. Avoid them when you can. When you can't avoid them, keep them short and follow a strict agenda.

- Schedule a time and place to handle physical mail and email when you are in the right frame of mind and have the right tools available.

- Keep the email you send short and to the point.

- Never ever, send an email when you are angry or when you have not first carefully proofed it to make sure it says what you want to say in the way you want to say it. When in doubt about sending an email, don't send it.

- Always assume that every human being and machine on earth can view and read any email you send and that no email will ever be completely deleted.

114….Joseph H. Boyett & Jimmie T. Boyett

CHAPTER FIVE: GET AND STAY ORGANIZED

The average person spends an estimated 150 hours—the equivalent of 19 working days—every year searching for information or items they need to get their work done but somehow have misplaced.

(Haddock 2001, pp. 64-65.)

In this concluding chapter, we are going to discuss an approach to getting organized developed originally by Japanese manufacturers but the approach applies equally well in any workplace. It is called the 5S Process.

5S is an abbreviation for the five Japanese words that are the steps to getting organized.

- **Seiri (Sort)** —Sort through items in your work area and remove anything that is unnecessary.

- **Seiton (Set in Order)** —Place all the necessary items in their place where they will be easily accessible when needed.

- **Seiso (Shine)** —Keep everything clean, neat and orderly.

- **Seiketsu (Standardize)** —Create standards for Sorting, Setting in Order, and Shining so that the cleanliness of the workplace is maintained.

- **Shitsuke (Sustain)** —Have self-discipline; don't backslide. Make the 5S's a way of life.

(Primary source for 5S Process: Fabrizio & Tapping 2006)

The idea behind the 5S process is that you will be more productive if you arrange your workplace so "there is a place for everything and everything is in its place." You'll spend less time looking for the things you need to get work done and consequently you will get more done.

Let us look at each of the five steps in the 5S process.

NOTE: Patricia Haddock, author of *The Time Management Workshop*, says you should not try to organize your life all at once. After all, you did not get disorganized in one day. In addition, getting organized takes time—time that you don't have. That's why you are reading this book. Instead of trying to fix your disorganization all at once, Haddock says you should start by just devoting a few minutes to your organization task. Even if you spend only 15 minutes working on the 5S process that we discuss here, 15 minutes here and there will add up over time and yield big benefits in time management and efficiency. Haddock says most people can gain quick benefits by starting with their immediate work area, their desk or their workspace. Others can gain the quickest benefits from tackling a storage area they use frequently. It is less important where you start, says Haddock, than that you start somewhere. Even if you just start with one desk drawer or one shelf, JUST START.

(Haddock 2001, pp. 64-65)

STEP ONE: SORT

You begin the 5S process by literally cleaning up your workplace. You can do this by yourself or get a colleague to help.

ESTABLISH A "HOLDING AREA."

This is a place, box, container, storage closet, etc. where you and/or others will place things identified as unnecessary. The holding area should be clearly marked and used only for temporary storage of items considered no longer needed. Keep items in the holding area for three to four months. If no one has needed them after that time, donate them to someone who can use them or discard them. Decide who will be responsible for maintaining the holding area and disposing of items after they have reached their time limit.

Purchase some red tags or stickers to place on each item you decide is unnecessary indicating when you placed it in the holding area and when it can be disposed of if not used.

Walk through your work area looking for items that you no longer need. Examine each item in your work area—equipment, paper, etc. Ask yourself:

- Do I need this item to perform my work? Place a RED tag/sticker on unnecessary items.

- If I need it, is it needed in this quantity or could I do with less?

- If I need it, how frequently do I use it?

- If I don't use it frequently, does it need to be here or could I move it to some other storage location? If so, where?

- Who is ultimately responsible for maintaining this item? Is it me or someone else? If so, who?

- Are there any other items in my workspace that I don't need?

- Are there any tools, material, equipment that I need but are left lying on a table or on the floor rather than in their proper place? What is their proper place?

Haddock says you may want to make a checklist of these questions you can use as you examine each item for sort and toss.

(Haddock 2001 pp. 64-76)

Haddock says you are not finished with your sort and toss session until you have disposed of every item. Everything that you need to keep should be in its proper location or file. Everything you don't need or can easily replace needs to go in the trash or be disposed of appropriately. For example, you should shred paper documents that contain sensitive information.

Move all RED tagged items to the holding area. If you are not sure whether an item is necessary or not, place a different colored tag on it and segregate it from other items in the holding area.

Consider having two holding areas, one for your workspace and another "company" holding area. When items reach their time limit in your holding area, move them to the "company" holding area for a designated period before final disposal.

STEP TWO: SET IN ORDER

Your next step in getting organized is to make sure all necessary items are in their proper place and available for easy access.

CLASSIFY ALL NECESSARY ITEMS BY FREQUENCY OF USE:

- Place items or equipment used hourly or daily within arm's reach at your workspace.

- Place items or equipment used weekly or once a month in a storage location near your work area.

- Place items or equipment used less often in a distant storage location

Move all necessary items to their proper location— arm's reach, work area storage, distant storage according to their frequency of use.

Make a list of items contained in storage lockers, cabinets, or other containers and post the list on the front of the locker or cabinet or shelf where the container is located.

Use markers to outline the proper storage location of items. For example, outline where people should hang a tool on a pegboard. Use labels, pictures, diagrams and so on to...

- Define aisle ways that must be kept open,

- Show the proper position and location of equipment,

- Indicate the range of swing that must be kept free for open doors, etc.
- Draw attention to safety hazards,
- Show direction

Use color-coding to convey information rapidly to yourself and others. For example,

- GREEN—Location of safety equipment, first aid kits, etc.
- RED—Location of firefighting equipment.
- YELLOW/ORANGE—Cautions, warnings

ORGANIZE YOUR PAPER DOCUMENTS

Create files using broad headings. Use different codes for different broad headings and subcategories. You can label according to subject, alphabetically, geographically, chronologically, or numerically as long as you follow one consistent method when creating new categories. Create a Master List of your file main headings and sub-categories with cross-references.

Keep files you use frequently near your work area, and archive files you rarely use.

Periodically conduct a Sort and Toss session for each file drawer. Jan Yager recommends you do this on the first workday of each month, quarter and year.

Julie Morgenstern says you should ask yourself the following questions about each document you find in your workspace:

- Are there tax or legal reasons to keep it?

- Do I refer often to this piece of paper?

- Will it help me complete a project I am working on right now?

- Do I have time to do anything with this piece of paper?

- Does it tie in with the core activities of my job?

- Do I trust that the information is up to date?

- Does it represent a viable business opportunity?

- Will it help me make money?

- Would my work suffer if I did not have it?

- If I ever needed it again, would it be hard to find or recreate?

If you answer YES to any of these questions, keep the document; otherwise toss it.

(Morgenstern 2004, pp. 155-161)

Keep personnel files confidential, with access restricted to authorized people only.

Set up a Tickler File. Set up a file for each day of the month so that you have 31 file folders and/or electronic files. Place items in the file for the day of the month in which you need to work on them. For example, "bills to pay" on the 15th.

Stop accumulating paper. Use these tips to cut out paper:

- Use the phone, electronic files, and email, whenever possible.

- Never put down a piece of paper without doing something to move it along.

- Create files only as needed using the criteria established in this section.

- Send copies to only those people who really need them.

- Set up a place for incoming mail and paper. Empty this in-basket daily using the sort and toss method.

- Set up a "to-file" box and empty it daily.

- Return files to their drawers promptly.

(Source, except as noted: Haddock 2001, p. 68)

ORGANIZE YOUR ELECTRONIC FILES

Regina Leeds offers the following tips for organizing your electronic files:

- Delete files you don't need. Old information is going to clog up the computer and make it run slower. Some companies have an electronic archive on a different server. Take advantage and store completed projects there. Use the cloud for backup

- If you use Windows, use the Documents feature. If you place all of your files in the standard Documents folder, they will be easier to find and easier to backup.

- Create categories so you can keep related information in the same place. Use the same main categories you use for paper files.

- Create a large folder and place individual subject-matter related files inside. Keep file names short but memorable. If you can, color-code file folders on your hard drive with the same color you use for related paper files in your filing cabinet.

• Use shortcuts when you need to access files from different locations instead of making multiple copies.

• Don't clutter your main screen with too many documents. Save that page for the files and programs to which you truly need a shortcut.

(Leeds 2009, p. 195)

STEP THREE: SHINE

Thoroughly clean your entire workspace. This requires more than just a simple sweeping and dusting. Use proper cleaning supplies to remove all dust, dirt, debris, and other contaminates. Turn your work area into a clean and bright place where you will enjoy working.

Obtain appropriate cleaning supplies and place them in a container so they will be close and handy. Determine who will be responsible for checking and replenishing these supplies as needed.

Make cleaning/shining a daily activity. Clean your work area before you start working on any project and once again when you finish work on a project. Set aside at least 10 to 15 minutes each day to devote to nothing but Shine.

Develop a written schedule for maintenance of equipment and in depth cleaning that is required on a periodic basis to keep equipment in proper working order. Determine who will be responsible for this maintenance. Post the schedule along with the name of the person responsible.

You should create and follow a cleaning checklist so that you are sure that you perform all regular cleaning actions. For example, the checklist should specify the maintenance process for inspecting and cleaning a piece of equipment on a regular basis.

During cleaning check and inspect every item to insure that it is in proper working order. Replace or repair any broken items. Clean both the inside and outside of work areas. Identify and tag every item that can cause contamination.

Keep a log to record ideas for cleaning improvements. Record…

- Where the clean problem occurs.

- What the cleaning problem is exactly.

- Who should be responsible for taking action to correct the problem.

- When (how soon) a solution to the problem should be found and implemented.

- How critical is it to find an immediate solution?

Yager says the key to organizing/shining your workspace is to "have at hand everything you need, but not more than you need." For example, he says make sure you have enough supplies (pens, paper, pencils, tape, stapler, etc.) but not more than you need. Extra supplies should be stored in a supply closet away from your work area. Add things such as a picture of your kids that make your workspace attractive and pleasant, a place you want to be. Remove items that will distract you for the task at hand such as a picture from your last vacation that prompts daydreaming or a toy that you just can't resist playing with." Yager warns that you should have out on your desk or in view only those items, records or data that you really need for the task you are working on at the time. If you have out items for other projects, you will be tempted to jump from one project to the next. Take out what you need for the task and ONLY what you need.

(Yager 1999, pp. 79-82.)

STEP FOUR: STANDARDIZE

Check to see that the first three S's have been performed properly. Establish routines and standard practices for repeating the first three S's regularly and systematically. Create and distribute written forms, procedures and checklists for performing and evaluating the performance of the first three S's.

STEP FIVE: SUSTAIN

Encourage everyone in your workplace to follow the Five S's. Everyone in the workplace should treat it the way they would their home. Regularly check to see that the first four S's have been done and graphically display the results on a board to give everyone feedback and reinforcement for their 5S performance. Reward yourself and others for each month you sustain the Five S's with a 5S celebration luncheon or treat.

(Source: Except where noted, Tapping 2006)

KEY IDEAS

Use the 5S process to get and stay organized.

SORT

(Remove unnecessary items)

SET-IN-ORDER

(Place all necessary in their place.)

SHINE

(Keep everything clean, neat and orderly.)

STANDARDIZE

(Create standards for sorting, setting-in-order and shining.)

SUSTAIN

(Have self-discipline, Make the 5S's a way of life.)

CHAPTER SIX: SUSTAIN

In Chapter One, we said that the first thing to learn about time management was that you really could not manage time. You could only manage your use of time. Time management, we said, was really about YOU MANAGEMENT OR WHAT YOU DO NEXT MANAGEMENT.

We discussed the 5S process for getting organized in the last chapter. The last step in that process, as you will recall, was Sustain. Sustain is perhaps the key step in the implementation of the 5S process. If you don't sustain 5S, if you don't Sort, Set-In-Order, Shine, and Standardize repeatedly, any benefits you derive from completing the 5S process the first time will be quickly lost. Your workspace will become disorganized once again.

Sustaining 5S is the key to staying organized. Sustaining is the key also to time management in general. Managing your time is like going on a diet. No matter how great the diet and how much weight you take off, you will gain it all back if you don't change your eating and exercise habits. Like dieting to lose weight, in the end time management is all about changing your daily habits to gain better control over the tasks and activities you perform each day. We hope you have started that process.

We hope that you didn't just READ this book. We hope you APPLIED the ideas in this book. We hope you did several of the goals exercises in Chapter two and have defined several SMART goals for your personal and professional life. We hope you didn't just read about time logs, but actually kept one for a week or longer. We hope you analyzed your log and identified your time wasters. We hope you have started keeping a daily To-Do list and that updating your To-Do list is now a regular part of your daily routine. We hope you are setting priorities for items on your To-Do list and that you have purged it as much as possible of activities that aren't related to your Big Picture SMART goals. We hope you now have a better idea why you procrastinate and that you are having a lot less trouble eating those ugly frogs. We hope you actually kept an interruptions log and discovered what was causing your BAD interruptions and that you have stopped them or, at least, greatly reduced their frequency. We hope you are delegating more, saying "NO" more, conducting and/or attending better meetings and, most importantly, avoiding meetings you do not need to attend. We hope you are handling physical mail and email more efficiently. Finally, we hope you have sorted, set-in-order, shined, and standardized. We hope you have put to work the excellent advice of our time management gurus that we summarized in this book and that you will read some of our gurus' books for more time management tips.

Now, you have one more critical task ahead of you, the most important time management task of all…..

Sustain!

ABOUT THE AUTHORS

JOSEPH H. BOYETT, Ph.D., is an accomplished author and leadership consultant/speaker who specializes in helping people understand and implement state-of-the art management and leadership practices to improve their personal and professional lives. He has been a consultant to executives at a number of Fortune 500 companies including IBM, BP, Merck, EDS, Sara Lee/Hanes and BellSouth. Dr. Boyett is the author of nineteen previous books and hundreds of articles on leadership and management, including *Workplace 2000, Beyond Workplace 2000*, the five-volume *Guru Guide* series, and *Won't Get Fooled Again: A Voter's Guide to Seeing Through the Lies, Getting Past the Propaganda, and Choosing the Best Leaders*. Dr. Boyett holds a Ph.D. in Political Science from the University of Georgia and is a member of The Author's Guild, the American Political Science Association, and the American Society of Journalist and Authors (ASJA). Publishers have translated his books into more than a dozen languages. Dr. Boyett lives in Alpharetta, Georgia, outside Atlanta, with his wife and co-author Jimmie. You can contact Dr. Boyett through his website at http://www.jboyett.com.

JIMMIE T. BOYETT is a consultant, trainer and the co-author of the *Guru Guide* series and four other books on management and leadership. Ms. Boyett holds a Master's Degree in Education and is the founder and President of the distance learning company Training On Demand, LLC. You can contact her through her company's website at http://ectod.com

130....Joseph H. Boyett & Jimmie T. Boyett

OTHER BOOKS BY THE AUTHORS

OTHER GURU GUIDES BY THE AUTHORS

The Guru Guide

The Guru Guide to Entrepreneurship

The Guru Guide to the Knowledge Economy

The Guru Guide to Marketing

The Guru Guide to Money Management

OTHER BOOKS BY THE AUTHORS

Beyond Workplace 2000

Team Tools Handbook

The Gainsharing Design Manual

The Skill-Based Pay Design Manual

OTHER BOOKS BY JOSEPH H. BOYETT

Guidebook to Georgia County Government

Judicial Administration in Georgia

Handbook for Georgia Mayors and Councilmen

Maximum Performance Management

132....Joseph H. Boyett & Jimmie T. Boyett

The Competitive Edge

Workplace 2000

The Quality Journey

Won't Get Fooled Again

Getting Things Done in Washington

The Science of Leadership

BIBLIOGRAPHY

Allen, D. (2001). *Getting Things Done: The Art of Stress-Free Productivity.* New York: Penguin Books.

Ettus, S. (2008). *The Expert's Guide to Doing Things Faster.* New York: Crown.

Emmett, R. (2009). *Manage Your Time to Reduce Your Stress.* New York: Walker & Company.

Fabrizio, T and D. Tapping (2006). *5S for the Office: Organizing the Workplace to Eliminate Waste.* New York: Productivity Press.

Felton, S and M. Sims (2009). *Organizing Your Day: Time Management Techniques That Will Work for You.* Grand Rapids, Michigan: Revell.

Griessman, B. E. (1994). *Time Tactics of Very Successful People.* New York: McGraw-Hill.

Haddock, P. (2001). *The Time Management Workshop: A Trainer's Guide.* New York: AMACOM.

Hallowell, E. M. (2006). *Crazy Busy: Overstretched, Overbooked, and About to Snap!* New York: Ballantine/Random House.

Hoover, J. (2007). *Time Management: Setting Priorities to Get the Right Things Done.* New York: Harper Collins.

Leeds, R. (2009). *One Year to an Organized Work Life: From Your Desk to Your Deadlines, the Week-by-*

Week Guide to Eliminating Office Stress for Good. Philadelphia, PA: De Capo Press.

Luecke, R. (2005). *Time Management: Increase Your Personal Productivity and Effectiveness.* Boston: Harvard Business School Publishing.

Mackenzie, A. (1997). *The Time Trap, Third Edition.* New York: AMACOM and Mackenzie, A. and Pat Nickerson (2009). *The Time Trap, Fourth Edition.*

Merritt, C. (2009). *Too Busy for Your Own Good: Get More Done in Less Time--with Even More Energy.* New York: McGraw-Hill.

Morgenstern, J. (2004). *Making Work Work: New Strategies for Surviving and Thriving at the Office.* New York: Fireside/Simon & Schuster.

Prentice, S. (2005). *Cool Time: A Hands-on Plan for Managing Work and Balancing Time.* New York: John Wiley.

Roesch, R. (1998). *Time Management for Busy People.* New York: McGraw-Hill.

Silber, L. (1998). *Time Management for the Creative Person.* New York: Three Rivers Press.

St. James, E. (2001). S*implify Your Work Life: Ways to Change the Way You Work So You Have More Time to Live.* New York: Hyperion.

Tracy, B. (2007). *Eat That Frog! -21 Great Ways to Stop Procrastinating and Get More Done in Less Time.* San Francisco: Berrett-Koehler Publishers.

Tracy, B. (2007). *Time Power: A Proven System for Getting More Done in Less Time Than You Ever Thought Possible.* New York: AMACOM.

Tullier, M. (2000). *The Complete Idiot's Guide to Overcoming Procrastination.* Indianapolis, IN: Alpha Books.

Wetmore, D. E. (2005). *The Productivity Handbook: New Ways of Leveraging Your Time, Information and Communication.* New York: Random House.

Yager, J. (1999). *Competitive Time Management for the New Millennium.* Stamford, CT: Hannacroix Creek Books.